Mark Williams

LORRAINE McGEE-SIPPEL is a descendant of the Yorta Yorta people from the Murray-Goulburn region on the Victorian-NSW border. Born in 1943, Lorraine spent her childhood years in rural NSW and Sydney. She worked in a variety of jobs after she left high school, and in her late twenties she took up a career in nursing.

Lorraine began writing in the 1990s and her work has appeared in numerous anthologies and publications. Her manuscript 'Hey Mum, What's a Half-Caste?' was twice shortlisted for the David Unaipon Award. In 2008 she received the Inaugural Yabun Elder of the Year Award for her contribution to Reconciliation and Community Work.

Hey Mum, What's a Half-Caste?

LORRAINE McGEE-SIPPEL

This is a Magabala Book

LEADING PUBLISHER OF ABORIGINAL AND TORRES STRAIT ISLANDER STORYTELLERS.

CHANGING THE WORLD, ONE STORY AT A TIME.

Aboriginal and Torres Strait people are advised that this publication contains names and images of deceased persons. Approval has been obtained from the appropriate people to publish these names and images.

First published in 2009, reprinted 2009.
Reprinted with revisions 2017, 2019, 2020, 2021
Magabala Books Aboriginal Corporation
1 Bagot Street, Broome, Western Australia
Website: www.magabala.com Email: sales@magabala.com

Magabala Books receives financial assistance from the Commonwealth Government through the Australia Council, its arts advisory body. The State of Western Australia has made an investment in this project through the Department of Local Government, Sport and Cultural Industries. Magabala Books would like to acknowledge the generous support of the Shire of Broome, Western Australia.

Magabala Books is Australia's only independent Aboriginal and Torres Strait Islander publishing house. Magabala Books acknowledges the Traditional Owners of the Country on which we live and work. We recognise the unbroken connection to traditional lands, waters and cultures. Through what we publish, we honour all our Elders, peoples and stories, past, present and future.

Cover Design Jo Hunt
Printed and bound by Ovato Print Pty Ltd

9781921248030 (paperback)

A catalogue record for this book is available from the National Library of Australia

In memory of my Yorta Yorta grandmother,
Dinah Myrtle Wooding (nee McGee),
who never stopped loving me, despite not knowing
where I was for the first thirty-eight years of my life.

My story is not just my story. There is a family to consider and I have changed some names to protect privacy. This is an account of my life as I remember it. People familiar with my story may have a different version. This is mine.

LORRAINE MCGEE-SIPPEL

Acknowledgements

Thank you to the people and organisations who have helped me on my journey—(Dr) Mick Asher who understood the importance of finding my family, Peter Bishop (Varuna, the Writers' House), Rob Pullen (ASA), Cousin Shirl, Aunty Pat for permission to use and expand on Joe's story, Peter Read, Susan Murphy for reading early drafts, Petrina Slaytor for help in searching for Fred, my biological father, my late friend Joan Whetton for introducing me to Link-Up, Oomera (Coral) Edwards for her guidance in those early visits to my ancestral country, Monica Morgan from Cummeragunga who told me I was a Yorta Yorta woman, and Jack Beetson for my introduction to Aboriginal culture. Thanks to (Dr) Wayne Atkinson for permission to use his map of Yorta Yorta Country as a reference, and to my late godson, Mark Williams, and Fiona Morris, for the author pic. We miss you, Mark.

Thank you to those Indigenous and non-Indigenous writers and humanists I have read with, listened to, and learnt from. Special thanks to (Dr) Anita Heiss, who has believed in me and my writing from the beginning. I do not know how to thank you enough, Anita. To Pearlie McNeill for making my words stand strong on the page and for her wonderful writers' group.

Thanks to (Dr) Janet Hutchinson who makes the editing process look so easy, and to Rachael Christensen and the mob at Magabala Books for the opportunity to tell my story.

I am ever grateful to my Yorta Yorta Elders and family who welcomed me into their hearts and homes, and who generously filled in the gaps from long ago.

Thank you to Moirs Bookshop, LCRFR (Lane Cove Residents for Reconciliation), WAIG (Lane Cove Women's Action and Information Group), Lane Cove Council, and to all my friends and supporters who have patiently waited for this day to arrive.

And, of course, to my dear husband Kevin, for his unwavering love and support.

Foreword

Anyone who has ever been called a 'half-caste' will understand the pain and torment such a phrase can inflict on a person, especially a child trying to understand what it means.

'Half-caste' suggests one is not whole or complete. And it is this phrase that had Lorraine McGee-Sippel start to realise her life and her ancestry were shrouded in mystery. As a young child she began a journey which would last decades and leave her 'emotionally disturbed' as she sought answers to the questions that plagued her heart and her mind.

The importance of family is a central theme throughout Lorraine's story—her biological family, her adoptive family and the family of friends she made along the way. We learn of the 'layers of confusion' that not only consumed her own life, but the lives of others like her, all searching for a belonging that can only be found from knowing where you have come from.

The raw honesty in Lorraine's words and her immeasurable generosity in baring her heart and soul will inspire readers. Lorraine tells us it is hard to convey how fraught the reconnection process is for an adopted person. Many of us, who know who we are and where we come from, may never fully understand Lorraine's story. Hers is a particular voice—one that should not invoke pity, but help you, as it did me, to learn more about yourself and the ways we can all be more compassionate.

Even as a child amid her own emotional trauma, Lorraine showed compassion. That compassion carried her through her career as an accomplished nurse and into her life today. It has seen her become one of the most respected elders in Sydney, and a fitting recipient of the Inaugural Yabun Elder of the Year Award in 2008.

Through a life of heartache, confusion and unknowing, Lorraine has emerged as a woman of substance and strength. She could be bitter about the missed stories of her family, the pieces of her siblings' lives that she will never know, but the woman affectionately referred to as

'Toots' by her adoptive father Allan, considers herself lucky to know some of her history at all.

Lorraine's journey is about her finding a way home—to her biological family, to her roots, to her country. As Lorraine says, 'This coming home was a cause for joy, anticipation, celebration and explanation.'

The final lesson in Lorraine's story is that we are a nation of strong people and regardless of categories and labels we will always be proud of who we are and what we have survived.

I am proud to say that this Yorta Yorta woman who goes by the name of Lorraine 'Toots' McGee-Sippel is in my family too.

DR ANITA HEISS, *author and cultural activist*

Prologue

The door of our fifteenth-floor balcony was open, ready for the southerly when it arrived. The day had been hot and I'd not long arrived home from work. I was so happy I was ready to burst, but Dad looked like he didn't know whether to laugh or cry. He stood up and began pacing the floor; he said he had something important to tell me. His voice was quietly serious but he was smiling.

'Sit down, Toots.'

My mother sat on the lounge, her headache manageable for the time being. She looked at Dad, then I looked at him too. What could be so important? And why did he have to tell me now? I had just told my parents the good news that I was getting married, but Dad already knew. Jack had come by earlier and they'd been up the street for a celebratory drink.

Dad cleared his throat, giving no warning of what was to follow.

'Toots…' he began. 'When we collected you from Scarba Home at Bondi, the social worker said we had to tell you something before you got married. Toots, your mother was white, but your father was black. He was a Negro. The social worker said we'd be sorry for taking you, and that you'd have to be checked out by a doctor before you had kids. She said you could have throwbacks and your husband might think you'd been playing around.'

I don't know if the shock was showing on my face but I do remember that my mouth was suddenly dry and I seemed to be having trouble hearing. Negro? Throwbacks? They'd be sorry for taking me?

'You see, Toots, no-one else wanted you, but Mum and I did.'

I slumped forward on the lounge like a wounded animal, unable to move.

'What's the matter, Lorraine?' Mum asked. 'Lorraine, what's the matter?'

She kept asking the same question over and over again, like a record needle stuck in a groove, her voice rising with each word.

Allan spoke like a man on a mission.

'You'll have to tell Jack,' he said, sliding the phone across the table towards me.

Half-Caste

'You half-caste,' he hissed in my ear, as he walked past and bumped my wooden stool.

I thought he was joking, that he'd laugh or say something funny but he didn't. No-one, not our teacher Mr McDonald who was standing near the blackboard, or anyone else seemed to hear what Wally had just said.

School at Isis River was good until he arrived. Ours was a one-room, one-teacher school, with twelve kids that year, aged between six and fifteen. Teachers' contracts were for two years and the best years for me were 1951 and 1952 when Mr McDonald came. I liked him because he smiled and laughed. He made learning fun as well as interesting.

By the time I got home that afternoon Mum was in the kitchen starting tea.

'I don't want to go back to school tomorrow,' I told her.

'Why not?'

'Just don't.'

Mum and I didn't talk a lot. I seemed to get on her nerves, so

I had to be careful when I said anything. She didn't like me being silly, telling lies or spreading tales.

I wasn't sure what to say next, because if I asked Mum what a half-caste was, she might think I was trying to get Wally into trouble. I didn't want to get anyone into trouble, but especially Wally. We were in the same class and had to sit next to each other. I only wanted to know what the word meant.

Mum was standing at the sink, facing me. She had a knife in one hand and a potato in the other, waiting, frowning.

'Hey Mum, what's a half-caste?'

'Who said that?'

Her voice was shaky, and she avoided looking at me by turning back to the sink, back to the vegetables.

I was sitting opposite, watching her. Whatever it was that was making her act so strangely, seemed to have something to do with me—and that word, whatever it meant.

The next day Wally was given six strokes of the cane, and I remember feeling guilty for dobbing him in. We only spoke when we had to after that. At least no-one called me a half-caste again. But I still didn't know what the word meant.

My family—Mum (Flo), Dad (Allan) and me—lived then on Waverley Station, a sheep and cattle property run by Mr and Mrs Crane.

Waverley was on the Gundy Road, twenty-five miles from Scone in the Hunter Valley of New South Wales.

My best friend, Richard, was a year younger than me; he used to call for me every school day.

'Ya there, Rainee?' he'd yell. Sometimes he'd add Annie, my second name.

Mr and Mrs Crane were Richard's grandparents. He lived with them during the week and went home to his parents at Blandford on weekends. Blandford was further out, about twenty-five miles away on the Timor Road near Murrurundi.

Like me, Richard was an only child although he used to have a little brother called Tommy who had white hair. Tommy couldn't hear or speak; he was four when he died. Mum said that before that he was in a special school, down in Sydney.

For as long as I could remember, I pestered Mum for a baby sister. I didn't like being an only child. It was too lonely. Some people thought I was spoilt, but I wasn't. Mum made sure of that. Dad reckoned she was too hard on me. Anyway, she said something about not being able to have any more children. It was very disappointing for all of us.

~

Isis River School was about half a mile from home on the other side of the river. Most days we walked across a low-level, wooden bridge to get there but one day it rained so much Mr McDonald said we couldn't go home because the river was in flood. We couldn't even go outside to look. Instead, five of us were told we'd be staying at Mr and Mrs Sullivan's place for the night.

Mr Sullivan worked for Mr Crane's son on another property, and his wife collected our mail and bread three days a week from Gundy, thirteen miles away. The three Sullivan children were at school with us, and their house was over the hill and across the bridge from ours. Daryl, a year younger than me, started crying at this news. He wanted to go home.

'It's all right, we'll go tomorrow,' I said, holding his hand as we were lifted onto the back of a cattle truck in the pouring rain.

All the time I was trying not to be scared myself. I'd never slept away from home before.

Mrs Sullivan already had a number of mattresses on the floor and a log fire going by the time we arrived. She helped us towel ourselves dry and lent us fresh clothes while ours were strung out to dry. Soon we were sitting up at the big wooden table in the kitchen with bowls of bread and hot milk. It was so yummy. I wanted to stay with the Sullivan family forever.

One day, not long after the flood, I overheard Mrs Crane remarking to Mum what a good daughter she had.

'She's a real little mother the way she conducts herself and looks after the younger children,' she was saying in her posh, gravelly voice.

Whenever I saw Mrs Crane after that she'd ask, 'How's Waverley's little mother?'

I couldn't help smiling. Her words made me feel important.

Mrs Crane was generous in other ways too. When she bought something for Richard she'd buy something for me as well. Richard spent more time at our place than theirs because there were no children for him to play with at the homestead.

'You'll have to start charging him board soon,' Mrs Crane would say to Mum, with a wink. 'Do send him home if he doesn't behave himself.'

I loved Richard's family; they weren't snobs like some property owners. Mum reckoned too much money resulted in snobbery. She used to say money was a curse if you had it and a curse if you didn't. We could have done with a bit more ourselves though, to pay Mum's doctor's bills. She got headaches that wouldn't go away, no matter how many Bex and Vincents Powders she managed to swallow. She would cry and be very cranky. She could also lash out without warning.

I remember being hit when I was about three years old. I had been poking my tongue out, to see how far it would go. I wasn't being cheeky but Mum said I was. Her hand came rushing towards me and caught me just under the chin. It hurt so badly I couldn't stop crying. My tongue became ulcerated where I had bitten it and my parents had to take me to see the doctor. He was cross and told Mum she was not fit to be a mother. My father, playing the peacemaker, did what he could to smooth things over. But I had learned a valuable lesson: keep out of Mum's way as much as possible. Her unpredictability knew no bounds.

One day, before I was old enough to go to school, I was playing with my trucks on the dirt track when a shadow cast over me. I looked up, and searched my mother's face as she bent towards me. My grip tightened on the trucks.

'You have to learn to share what you have with those who are less fortunate than yourself,' she said.

She told me she wanted to give my trucks to some little boys who had nothing. She'd already spoken to their mother.

My trucks. Mummy was taking them. She pulled at my fingers, tugging the trucks from my grip. I never saw those trucks again.

This was the first of many occasions when Mum's generosity, if that's what it was, cost me the loss of my precious possessions. She complained to Dad that whenever we had visitors I would disappear. I'd gone to hide my toys and books.

~

By contrast, life with Dad was mostly easier and less complicated. He called me 'Toots' and almost as soon as I could walk, I followed him everywhere. Whereas Mum's face was full of frowns, Dad's was all smiles. He called himself a 'country bumpkin'.

Born and bred in Kurri Kurri in the Maitland area of the

Hunter Valley, Dad was the eldest son of a second marriage, nine children in all. He spoke often of the poverty; four boys to a bed waking cold and wet most mornings, with never enough to eat and rumbling tummies.

His father was a carpenter, a strict disciplinarian who ruled by the strap that held his trousers up. Dad never spoke ill of his father, who was a good man and worked hard. It was their mother who got the boys into trouble, according to Dad.

'She'd be sweatin' on Dad every day after work, so she could tell on us. I wanted to learn to be a butcher but it cost money we didn't have. So I had to leave school and get a job at thirteen years of age. I was only a kid, Toots.'

I didn't know how old Mum and Dad were, but they didn't look any older than other kids' parents at school. Mum said it was none of my business anyway and that I should stop asking.

At five foot five, Dad was considered short for a man, but I never thought of him in that way. As far as I was concerned my father was someone to look up to, and to laugh with—and there was plenty of laughter, especially at night.

Dad had ears like jug handles, and I couldn't resist decorating them. There he would be, lolling back in his wicker chair, mirror in hand, admiring and laughing at himself. He didn't mind what was dangling or hanging off him, whether it was beads, ribbons or my favourite blue purse with the gold chain, just so long as he could have a laugh. Sometimes, we would catch Mum smiling.

'You're mad, the both of you,' she'd say, shaking her head and acting as if she were above all this silly carry-on.

Dad had told Mum that he went bald at seventeen. The little hair that remained was black, and he combed the strands across the shiny parts of his head. He wore a big sombrero when working outside so he didn't get sunstroke. His brother-in-law used to call Dad 'Baldie' every chance he got. I hated seeing Dad hurt. I don't know why he didn't tell Uncle Ernie off. Mum would have, if he'd called her names. She knew how to stick up for herself.

My mother was brought up in Marrickville in Sydney, close to the city and the local picture show, and she soon developed a passion for the Hollywood stars. She could rattle their names off as if she knew them personally. And perhaps in a way, she did. I thought her very clever. She played cards as well, and won prizes at euchre. She was the smart one in our family, and the boss.

The third eldest, and eldest girl in a family of seven children, her father used to say he could always rely on Florence. But boy, did she have a temper—and a mind of her own. She was very close to her father and used to write his business letters for him. Grandfather worked for Marrickville Council and Mum said that he was always doing good deeds for people in the community. He was a kind, softly spoken man and wore a built-up boot. Mum said he'd slipped on a banana skin, but I never knew if she was joking. Grandfather died when I was six years old. I remember Mum crying, and me crying because I didn't know how to stop her tears.

At the age of twenty, Mum left home to live with a boyfriend. Said she was sick of having to take her younger sister with her every time she went out. She wasn't a babysitter.

I wonder now what Nanna made of Mum's living arrangements. It was the late 1920s, and my grandmother was a Salvation Army woman. Good girls didn't live with their boyfriends before they married. Not in those days they didn't.

It was 1934 when Mum and Dad met and married. They worked on the same property and had known each other for six weeks. My mother worked as a domestic, while my father was the gardener and general hand. Who would have believed that this outgoing, attractive, well-dressed young woman would end up in the bush, being paid to do other people's dirty washing?

Nine years after their marriage, my parents adopted me. In those early years they moved around a lot, chasing work on stations and factories and living in small towns such as Walgett and Premer, and Rockley near Bathhurst. We even moved down to Glebe in Sydney before finally settling on Waverley Station in the Hunter Valley in 1950.

By then I was seven years old, and trying to adjust to the little bush school with only eleven pupils. Of course the number of students varied from time to time because of the high turnover of farm labourers and families. In 1953 there were fifteen of us. I had come from Glebe Public where I'd been learning to read and write, but the teacher at Isis River, the one before Mr McDonald, acted as if reading and writing didn't matter to little kids and didn't bother to teach us.

Richard and I were the youngest at the school. I should have been in second class, but I didn't feel as if I were in any class because all Richard and I seemed to do was to draw, play with plasticine and practise writing on our slates. It was fun at first but it soon became boring. I couldn't see the point in going to school if I wasn't going to be learning anything.

Mum worked part-time in the homestead laundry, while Dad tended the garden, milked the cows and slaughtered the sheep that we ate. We were told often that the electricity would be coming 'next year' but in the meantime, everything had to be washed and rinsed by hand. White things had to be boiled in the copper. To wring out the last of the rinsing water, Mum had to feed each item through the mangle. I tried to help but when things kept getting caught in the rollers all I could do was giggle. Mum would chase me outside so she could get on with her work. But whenever she yelled, 'Git outta my sight ya little bastard' I knew where to go.

Dad was always pleased to see me. 'In trouble again, Toots?' he'd say, taking out his old handmade knife to peel me an apple cucumber. Dad was always there for me and I knew he was my best friend long before I even started school.

One afternoon after school, when I was eight and sick of getting into trouble, I decided to leave home. Wearing my favourite pink silk dress with purple flowers and carrying my wooden school case with something to eat and drink and a change of clothes inside, I walked into the kitchen and told Mum I was going. Maybe she didn't believe me because I was halfway down the hill to the homestead before she caught up with me.

'Where are you off to, Lorraine?'

'Somewhere I'm wanted and where I don't get into trouble all the time,' I told her.

Mum looked sad and put her hand on my shoulder. I don't remember what was said but Mum did act as if she was sorry and offered to carry my bag as we walked back home.

The Family Album

At the time I didn't really understand why or how but my view of the world had changed dramatically that day when Wally called me a half-caste. For a start my skin was browner than that of everyone I knew, except for Maxie Brown. Maxie was at Segenhoe School but I used to see him at Belltrees Sports Day in September each year. Maxie was good at everything—running, jumping, hurdling, even the broad jump. He broke all the records and made new ones.

When I was nine years old I recorded a time of 7.1 seconds over fifty yards and went to Sydney with Maxie and others to represent the Upper Hunter Valley, Small Schools Amateur Athletic Association. Back then 7.1 seconds was a record for ten-year-olds. Mr McDonald said I could be the next Marjorie Jackson, the Olympic runner who was known as the 'Lithgow Flash', after the NSW town in which she grew up. In August 1952, a month before our Belltrees sports day, she won two Olympic gold medals at the Helsinki Games. It was very exciting being compared to someone who everyone seemed to be talking about.

Mum took a photo of me clutching the maroon pennant that I won. She put the photo in her album. When no-one was around I would open up that page and stare at myself. I'd look at Mum's relatives, then back at me, but I always seemed darker. How could my skin be so different to my parents', to that of all my aunties, uncles and cousins? Whenever I thought she was in a good mood I pestered Mum about it, but she would walk away from me muttering that kids should be seen and not heard. It was her favourite saying.

There was one little boy at school, two years younger than me, who didn't look like his mum or dad either. John had dark hair and brown eyes, and they didn't. This puzzled me. I wanted to know why, so one day in the playground I asked one of the older kids.

'He's adopted, that's why.'

'What do you mean?' I asked.

'It means that his mum and dad aren't his real mother and father. They weren't able to keep him, so they gave him away.'

The words hit me like a lightning bolt. If John was adopted then I must be too.

Soon after, my mother's sister Aunty Esther and her daughter Mavis came to stay with us for the May school holidays. I liked Mavis. I was going to show her our family photo album and find out whether she knew anything about when I was little, but impatience was stewing inside me. The more I went over what

I wanted to say in my head, the less prepared I was when things didn't turn out as I planned.

My cousin and I were sitting on the front steps where we sat every morning to warm up. Winter was on its way, so Aunty Esther and Mum had both bought some wool to start knitting. They were standing behind Mavis and I, near the firewood box, checking the size of their knitting needles, pushing them one at a time through a metal gauge.

'Mum,' I asked in my sweetest voice, 'can I show Mavis your photo album?'

'Not that again.'

Behind me, I heard her loud sigh.

'All right, go and get the damn thing. You know where it is.'

We couldn't find any photos of Mavis so she quickly lost interest. But I was so steamed up I could've been a whistling kettle. The words burst out of me, I felt so clever and proud of myself, and thought that Mum would be proud of me too for working it out on my own.

'Hey Mum,' I asked, 'am I adopted?'

Mum and Aunty were still standing behind Mavis and me, checking their knitting needles, so I couldn't see their faces, but I now knew why I looked different.

'Who told ya that?'

The shaky tone of voice was familiar. But Mum didn't say I wasn't adopted. Her reaction both surprised and disappointed me.

She was supposed to be excited like I was, but she seemed angry. I didn't know why, but I wasn't going to let it spoil my discovery.

Doing My Best

In 1953 I was in fifth class. It wasn't a good year. Mr Cutman, our new teacher was a plain-looking man, and he had a voice that sounded like he had a peg on his nose. I found it hard to look at him because I kept thinking I would see the peg and laugh.

I also knew that if I looked at him or said his name it'd make him a real person and I didn't want him to be real. He said I was insolent for not looking at him when he spoke to me but all I could think about was wanting Mr McDonald to come back.

Mum said to give the new teacher a chance, but she didn't know about the times he threw chalk at me and accused me of not wanting to learn. As far as I was concerned, Mr Cutman kept picking on me. I had this idea that if I ignored him long enough, he'd have to leave and teach at another school. But of course he never did.

Instead, he had a meeting with Mum and Dad and said that I was making it difficult for him to teach. He told Mum that I didn't like him. Well, that was true but I hadn't mentioned this to anyone.

I had been trying hard to keep my feelings to myself, even though he kept me in almost every day after school to write lines.

No-one stopped to think that Mr Cutman didn't like me. It was obvious to me that he didn't, but I couldn't be sure why. Maybe it was because I wasn't a property owner's daughter, or perhaps it was because I had brown skin.

One day I decided to show him how fast I was at hurdling and running. I thought that if I impressed him enough, he might be nicer to me and maybe we could get along. At the next athletics training session, I put in my best effort and raced past two of the older girls. One of them was Joyce Lindsay, Mr Cutman's favourite. If I thought he was going to congratulate me, I was wrong. He didn't say a word.

That night Dad asked how training went. When I told him he had tears in his eyes.

'Just do your best, Toots. Remember what Mr McDonald told you.'

It was really because of Mr McDonald that I tried so hard at athletics. I ran everywhere. He had believed in me, and so I believed in myself. If I wanted to be a champion athlete like Marjorie Jackson, the 'Lithgow Flash', then I knew I would have to keep working at it.

One day on the way to school, three of us were crossing the bridge and daring each other to walk on the edge. The deepest part of Isis River was usually no more than a few feet, which was just as well because I lost my balance and fell to the water below. I could feel my bag banging against my knee as I toppled downwards. It wasn't just my bag, my tunic, and my shoes and socks that got wet. Inside my bag was my lunch and my homework, now all sopping.

When Richard called out to me, I was thrashing around in the water. All I could think about was the trouble I'd be in at home and at school. I dragged myself home to face Mum, vowing I'd never muck around on the bridge again.

In September, that year, at our annual sports day at Belltrees, I decided I was going to win another pennant. I'd already won the heat in the morning, but Dianne Rossington, my rival from Gundy, had also been training hard.

There we were, neck to neck, racing down the home stretch. Dianne suddenly pulled ahead of me and burst through the tape. It was her turn to be champion and what a champion girl she was. We congratulated each other. I was disappointed at not winning but pleased for Dianne and felt I acted like a good sport. Besides, I'd won the runner-up trophy and come first in the hurdles final.

So many things were happening, and I was getting into trouble, at home and at school. I was still running everywhere, but now for some reason, I kept having accidents and falling over. Dad said it was because I didn't look where I was going. Maybe I was just getting clumsy. Most times it didn't bother me until one day I scraped my knee so bad that it wouldn't stop bleeding. I hopped and limped my way home, crying but thankful that it wasn't far to go.

Mum didn't like the sight of blood, but that was all right because Dad had just arrived home from work. Poor Dad was always being called on to fix things up. Now it was my turn to be tended to.

'Running again, Toots?' he asked, shaking his head, before fetching a basin of salt water, cotton wool and dressings, and proceeding to bathe my knee.

Suddenly, my head spun from side to side and my mouth fell wide open. I didn't know what had happened until I heard my mother yelling.

'What did you hit her for?'

'To shut her up, that's why. She was gettin' on me nerves, with her grizzling.'

I was too stunned to move, or to cry out. Dad had never hit me before (and never did again), and the slap had come out of the blue. I remember him storming out of the room and slamming the door. My face was burning, and I had a sinking feeling in my stomach, as if something worse was about to happen. I felt like I was on my own and I couldn't trust anyone.

Not long after Belltrees Sports Day, Mum said she was sending me down to Sydney to finish primary school. There was no warning and no explanation. When Mum said something, she meant it. I can still remember how I took a step backwards; I really felt like I had been kicked in the guts. I was ten years old.

At first Mum had asked which aunt and uncle I wanted to stay with, but when I told her I preferred Aunty Joan and Uncle Fred, she announced that she'd decided upon Aunty Esther and Uncle Ernie in Marrickville. I'd have to make the best of it.

Aunty Esther and Uncle Ernie were a miserable pair, and my least favourite relatives. They were Dad's least favourite too. I was puzzled why Mum had bothered to ask, when her mind was already made up.

Of course I could always visit Aunty Joan and Uncle Fred. They had four children younger than me and lived with Nanna, Mum's mother, around the corner from Aunty Esther's place. Nanna was a widow, and had been for five years; that was when Aunty Joan and Uncle Fred went to live with her.

In bed that night I kept thinking what might be behind this decision to send me away. What had I done that was so bad? I bet Mr Cutman had something to do with it. He'd never liked me. Why couldn't he go to another school? He was the grown-up, I wasn't. People would be thinking I was a troublemaker, but it wasn't me who was making trouble. Anyone could see that.

Mum said I'd learn girly things at school in Sydney, like sewing and all those things that would help to make me a lady. But I'd have to behave myself, she warned, and not answer anyone back, otherwise I could end up in a girls' home. I didn't want to be a lady, or end up in a girls' home. Mum was always threatening me with something.

Leaving Isis River meant leaving everyone and everything I loved. How would I get on without Dad to talk to? Who would help Mum when she had a headache? And what about Richard and the others at school? Would they forget me? I wouldn't forget them, or the animals, or swimming in the river, or collecting the eggs and watching the cows being milked.

I would miss staying up late with Dad on Friday nights listening to the championship boxing on the wireless. Jimmy Carruthers was the champion, and our favourite. The commentator spoke so loud and fast I couldn't understand what he was saying but I would look at Dad's face for clues. If he smiled and punched the air, I knew that everything was all right. That's when I could relax and rest back on the pillow.

I'd miss many things, and many people, except of course that horrible Mr Cutman. I also wouldn't miss getting into trouble with Mum and Dad, or listening to them arguing. They often had blues during the week, but Sundays were the worst. On Sundays Mum refused to get out of bed before nine. She'd worked all week and was sleeping in, she'd tell us.

Dad didn't have that luxury; he had to be up when everyone else was still asleep. The cows needed milking, and then the rest of the day was his. All he wanted was bacon and eggs for breakfast. Surely that wasn't too much to ask, I'd hear him yelling. Next thing pots and pans would be bouncing off the walls, and Mum would be screaming. I'd take off and go climb a tree. I hated Sundays.

There was no use pleading or saying anything about wanting to stay at Isis River. Mum didn't want to listen. Her mind was made up. I kept the tears to myself, that's what my pillow was for. It took a while to get used to the idea of going to Sydney but once I did, I couldn't wait to leave. There was no point hanging around where I wasn't wanted.

All in Together

Flo and I were on our way south to Sydney, the big smoke. I had just kissed Allan goodbye at Scone Railway Station. One minute I was excited about leaving home, and the next I was scared and wiping tears away.

It took some time for me to settle in. I didn't know of anyone else my age who'd been sent away from home because they didn't get on with a teacher, or any other reason for that matter. I felt ashamed and embarrassed, and kept wondering if I'd be sent away from Marrickville as well.

My stomach was tight with worry the day I started at Chapel Street Public School. The sixth class teacher, Miss Holt, looked a cranky sort of a person, like Aunty Esther, but then she smiled. She told the class to make me feel welcome, and that I was from the country. I stopped worrying after that.

Although I kept thinking of home, the strong smell of gas in Marrickville reminded me that I wasn't there. Back in 1954 that smell was everywhere—and not helped either by confined spaces and tiny houses squashed closely together. Everything seemed to be covered in soot from the factories, cars and smoky chimney stacks.

Where were the trees, grass and gardens, I wondered. The park was on a road that followed the route of rattly trams on their way to Newtown, where Aunty Esther used to shop. There were so many people. I'd never seen so many people. Most of them were in a hurry and looked straight ahead, as if I wasn't there.

Ned, my eldest cousin was about to join the Army. He was waiting until his papers were processed and then he'd be off. He shared a room with his younger brother John, who was handsome and kind. John and I got on well, but his sister Mavis didn't seem to like either of us. Just when I thought I had her worked out, her mood changed.

There were only two bedrooms. Mavis slept in her parents' room and I slept on a camp stretcher in the lounge room. It was like a public thoroughfare, people coming and going. Every morning the stretcher had to be folded up and put away.

The outside toilet at Aunty Esther's was dark and box-like, with a wooden seat over a long drop. A choko vine, heavy with fruit, grew over the tin roof. Aunty cooked chokos for dinner every night, and expected us all to eat every mouthful.

Aunty Esther didn't have the phone on, so Flo and Allan wrote letters every second week to both Aunty and I, and put them in the same envelope addressed to Aunty Esther. Flo's writing was strong and beautiful to look at, like calligraphy. She spoke of more practical things such as school, and whether I'd made any friends, and if so what their names were. Allan's letters were scratchy and all over the place, but fun to read because he wrote as he talked, telling me about the animals and what was happening on the property. He found writing difficult. He blamed it on the accident he'd had months before when he was out milking.

I can still recall the morning of the accident when Allan came into my bedroom to say that he needed to go to Scone Hospital. There'd been a blackout, so he'd had to milk by hand. Allan had names for all his cows and Cherry remained his favourite, even after she sat on the bucket that morning and severed the top joint of his right middle finger.

Flo refused to sleep with him when he came home from hospital. She couldn't stand the smell of his finger. It was rotten, she said. He'd asked her to cut it off, because the top part was dangling by a bit of skin, but Flo refused and hid the scissors. Instead of being amputated, a plaster cast was applied, and that's how Allan ended up with a dud finger, and scratchy handwriting.

Cousin Mavis was three years older than me and liked dressing up, especially on Friday nights. We were allowed to go to the pictures as long as we went together. I was tall for eleven, and Mavis let me wear her clothes and her lipstick. She didn't want to be shown up by being with someone younger. I soon realised she had no friends. Still, I was trying to fit in, to do things Mavis wanted to do.

My lips were painted 'Poppy Red' the night we made our escape from Addison Road picture show. I had no idea where we were going. I did my best to keep pace with her but it was hard to walk in Mavis' very tight skirt. By the time I caught up, she was talking to two boys; they were discussing where to go. I knew where I wanted to go, and it wasn't with these boys.

Turning the corner, we collided with Aunty Esther. I was shocked but relieved. The boys took off and Mavis and I copped a tongue lashing. Not that I blamed Aunty for going off, but at the same time I felt hard done by. I didn't understand why I had to be roused on and not allowed out for a month when I hadn't done anything wrong. It wasn't me who was boy mad, but Mavis.

It wasn't long before I noticed Uncle Ernie was looking at me in an odd way. I used to catch him peering over the top of his glasses.

'My, you're growing up fast, aren't you?' he'd say, running his tongue across his lips.

He was creepy and I did my best to stay out of his way as much as possible.

Uncle Ernie's parents lived across the road. Living with them was Daisy, their unmarried daughter, and Rosie, a grand-daughter, who belonged to Daisy's sister. Uncle rarely visited his parents so I could be free of him when I went to their place. I liked them all very much. Daisy wore callipers on both legs and couldn't open her hands properly, but she did beautiful fancywork and crocheting.

Rosie was four years older than me and had a blue pushbike she didn't ride anymore. Flo said she would buy it for me. The price was set at six pounds. I'd been riding the bike for some weeks when Uncle Ernie's mother said they were still waiting for the money and that I had to give it back. I was too proud to ask Flo about it.

Around this time Aunty Esther received a telegram from the Housing Commission. A three-bedroom house had become available at Seven Hills. I was on the move once more and feeling miserable. Now I'd have to start all over again.

~

Seven Hills was like living in the bush. There was vacant land at the back of the house. Wooden pegs were hammered into the ground to mark out plots for more housing but kids kept pulling them out. We ran wild, enjoying the freedom. There was room to move and places to run. The fibro houses all looked the same and were on big blocks. Uncle Ernie bought chooks. Those that didn't lay eggs were destined to become Sunday dinner.

Mavis and I shared the third bedroom. Everything smelt new and clean except for the dunny down the back. The pan man came in the early hours once a week. The dunny didn't smell so bad if you put deodoriser in it, held your breath and didn't sit too long.

The nearest high school was at Parramatta. Mavis had to travel back and forth by steam train to finish second year. I completed primary school at Seven Hills. I was excited when I heard that my teacher was to be Mr McDonald. But it wasn't my Mr McDonald from Isis River. I was really disappointed. This Mr McDonald was the headmaster. He was old and wore braces and a suit. His task was to prepare us for high school. The very thought scared me but the last term of the year passed soon enough.

Christmas was coming. I'd be going home for six whole weeks. It was good knowing I'd survived my first year away. And being at home meant I wouldn't have to write any letters for six weeks.

My arrival coincided with Isis River School's end-of-year concert and Christmas party. It was great catching up with Richard again. Flo said once he started going to boarding school in the new year he'd have friends with money. Friends who didn't mix with the working class. But I knew differently. I was sure Richard would never forget me—we were like family. When it came to Richard, Flo didn't know what she was talking about.

The weeks flew by, my days full of doing all the things I loved. I managed to catch up with Mrs Crane and she was still interested in everything I said and did.

I followed Allan around the garden, moving hoses while he mowed lawns. Standing under the trellis, we shared freshly picked grapes or apple cucumbers and tomatoes from the veggie patch. We got to eat the best of everything on the spot.

My favourite job was putting the separator together in the dairy. This stopped the cream getting mixed up with the milk, so we could make butter. Sometimes Flo said I helped Allan too much. What she really meant was that I had to help her more so that she didn't feel left out. It was a balancing act, one I had difficulty with.

I didn't get to see Richard again during those holidays, except from a distance. We waved and smiled but I wasn't bothered, I knew we'd catch up eventually.

Before I knew it, the time had come for me to go back to Seven Hills and start high school. I tried not to think about what it would be like. I hurried over to Allan for one last hug and kiss. It would be ten weeks until I saw him again.

'C'mon,' said Flo, 'we hafta get on the train. Now.'

'All aboard,' said the stationmaster, waving his flag.

As the train jerked forward and slowly gathered speed, I hung out the window and waved until Allan was but a tiny speck. If only things could have stayed as they were. With each clickety-clack I could feel myself being pulled away from all that I loved.

A Difficult Year

The taxi driver pulled up close to the front gate. Flo turned in her seat and looked at me. Her eyes were big like saucers. In front of us was Parramatta Secondary Home Science School. There were classrooms everywhere, upstairs and downstairs. I would never find my way around this place.

Each time someone spoke to us about books or the uniform Flo wrote something down. Her list was getting longer and longer. I was worried about that list, how much it was all going to cost her. Would she give me up if I cost too much? She was already paying Aunty Esther thirty shillings a week to look after me, and her headaches were becoming more frequent. That meant more doctors' bills.

I decided I could save money by walking instead of catching the bus to and from Parramatta Railway Station. It wasn't that far, and besides, every threepence I saved would add up and could be put towards buying myself something special. In the beginning it was a promise I kept to myself, and in the end I didn't want to catch that bus anyway, not with girls who all seemed to know each other and giggled all the time.

Later that afternoon, Flo was showing me how to wear a suspender belt when Aunty Esther barged into the bedroom.

'You've got your friends,' she said, standing behind me in the doorway, noting the pink stain on my nylon petticoat.

Flo must have seen the look on my face because she began to laugh. She told me that the bleeding meant I was getting my monthly periods.

'Wear it like this,' she said, placing the torn-up sheet between my legs, then fastening it onto a piece of elastic with safety pins.

Flo and Aunty Esther were both smiling, looking at me to check I had the belt on right. I couldn't understand why this could make anyone happy. Mavis wasn't happy though. She got the sulks when she found out that I had my periods before her.

Uniform parade was once a week. Flo couldn't afford to buy everything at once, so I didn't have every item on her list but I was happy to be one of the crowd of twelve hundred girls. Shoulders back, eyes straight ahead, I stood in line behind the girl in front. I was ready to march. Suddenly, I was tapped on the shoulder by a prefect. She asked me to follow her and to stand in front of the quadrangle facing everyone. There were a few other girls standing and I had to join them. They looked as scared as I felt.

Miss McCabe, who had seemed so grandmotherly and kind when Flo and I first met her, now pulled the microphone towards her. Speaking loudly, she directed everyone's attention to the girls who took no pride in their school or uniform. I didn't want to believe that Miss McCabe was talking about us. I peered down at the ground, wishing it would open up, as the well-dressed girls marched past in step with the beat of the military-type music.

Wearing full uniform meant everything to Miss McCabe. It was about pride, she emphasised, throwing her head back.

'Pride, girls. I'd rather wear a pair of stockings with ladders in them, than no stockings at all.'

I wasn't aware at the time but each class earned or lost points according to the state of each student's uniform. A few of us were considered half-dressed. So, my class didn't get off to a good start. But before long I was in full uniform, like everyone else. I wanted to study music and start running again, but I didn't dare ask. Best not to get involved, unless it was compulsory or free.

During the next holidays I mentioned to Flo that some girls in my class were learning an instrument. Annoyed, she threw her hands in the air.

'Those girls are spoilt,' she yelled. 'Their parents have nothing better to do than waste their money.'

In those early months at high school, the dermatitis I used to get every summer flared up. I must have been allergic to the cream they gave me because my hands got covered in blisters. The blisters soon became infected and turned into big cracks that would bleed. Flo had to come down and take me to Parramatta Hospital.

The specialist ordered me off school for six weeks and prescribed another cream that was thick and hard to use. It had to be melted over a flame each morning before it became pliable. I lived in dread of this torture, and I can still remember the burning sensation as the cream was applied. It was as if my poor bloodied and smelly hands were being branded by a hot poker. It was hard to stay still while Flo or someone else in the family took it in turns to act as nurse. I felt like jobbing them. The pain was so bad all I could do was scream until they had finished.

I couldn't even bathe myself, so Flo had to. At twelve years of age this was very embarrassing, and I refused to cooperate unless Mum looked the other way.

A kind neighbour, Mrs Johnson, made me two pairs of mittens from her children's old singlets. I had to wear the mittens to bed because my hands were painted with a purple dye every night. I felt funny wearing them but at least they kept the bedclothes clean.

Nothing seemed to go right that year. Strange things began to happen. One morning I woke up wearing my best dress over the top of my pyjamas. I had been known to sleepwalk when I was younger, and now Mavis said I talked in my sleep. For some reason Aunty Esther acted as though this behaviour was an insult to her.

At school I failed three exams and got further and further behind. The work was too hard. I'd missed six weeks of school and couldn't keep up. I was a dunce.

At least I was learning to cook; it was compulsory in First Year. The teacher said I was the messiest cook she'd ever seen, but my apple dumplings were as good as anyone's, even if the pastry was a bit tough. I looked forward to testing them out on Flo and Allan, and I marked the days off the calendar, thinking of home.

Most times Uncle Ernie saw Aunty Esther and I off on the train, but these holidays, my first since starting high school, I was allowed to travel home on my own. In five and a half hours I'd be meeting my parents at Scone Railway Station.

One last blast on the whistle and we were on our way. As the train clattered along, past factories and backyards, my mind kept drifting to the plan forming in my head. I was sure Flo had something that belonged to me, a document of some kind that would tell me who I was. I didn't know what the words would say exactly, but I felt certain that adoption would be mentioned.

I don't remember anyone telling me these things, I just seemed to have figured it out on my own. And the more I thought about it, the more impatient I was to get home and start looking.

Order of Adoption

Flo was down the hill at the homestead doing the laundry and Allan was working in the garden. I looked out the front door to make sure neither of them was coming, and then made my way to their bedroom.

The furniture in my parents' bedroom, like that in the rest of the house, didn't belong to us, but Flo said we still had to care for it as if it were our own. The four-poster double bed, set high with its springy mattress, took up most of the room. On it lay my mother's pride and joy, a white crocheted bedspread, made by Nanna. Flo had paid her mother thirty pounds to make it. Having hoped it would one day be handed down to me as an heirloom, I was mortified to learn a few years later that Flo had sold it. It had taken Nanna three years, and a lot of love, to make this exquisite piece of work for her eldest daughter and I think she would have been very upset had she known what Flo had done.

My mother kept her papers—business papers, she called them—in the second-top drawer of the chest, in a special wooden box my father had made for her. I'd seen Flo tip the contents onto the bed often enough to know where they were kept. But the closer I moved towards the drawer, the more my stomach churned. I hated sneaking around like a thief but if she'd answered my questions I wouldn't have had to. The argument went back and forth in my head, but I wasn't about to let that stop me.

Opening the drawer, I held the knob with one hand while I poked around with the other, until my fingers touched something hard. The box. It was light and small. I slid the lid off and up-ended the contents onto the bedspread. My hands were sweating. I wiped them on my skirt.

There were four papers. I opened, then folded, three of them. They seemed important—one was a birth certificate—but not what I was looking for. Hopefully this last document would be the one.

I opened it. It smelt musty and was a creamy colour, bigger in size and thicker than the others. Somehow that seemed to make it even more important. I read the words—Order of Adoption. I stared at the paper, my eyes blurring so much I couldn't read properly. I knew right away this had to do with me. There were so many words on that paper, too many to read in a hurry. I couldn't understand some of them. I was trying my best.

What time was it, I wondered. I wasn't wearing a watch. Flo would be home soon. I could hear the alarm clock ticking on Allan's side of the bed, but the paper in my hand was too important to leave. Every second was precious.

Under the main heading there were two names printed in big letters. One was my name, Lorraine, then my surname. And then there was another name. Gloria Wooding. I'd never heard of her. The date on the document was 28 May 1943. I was born that January, so I must have been four and a half months old when this was typed up.

Down further, on the left-hand side, I could see my parents' names, their occupations and an address in Marrickville. I knew they had lived in Marrickville when I was a baby.

I was beginning to feel dizzy with all those words swirling in my head. I used to be Gloria? Had my name been changed to Lorraine? Could I call myself Gloria when I got sick of being Lorraine? But I liked Lorraine better. So who were my real mother and father? And where were their names? I couldn't see anything to even give me a clue. Is that what happened when you were adopted, you got two names? Oh damn, the screen door was banging. I could hear footsteps. They had to be Flo's. This was the time she returned from the laundry after hanging the washing out. If it was anyone else they would have banged loudly on the screen door before calling out.

'Where are you, Lorraine?'

I folded the paper quickly but there was no time to put it back. Flo was already bursting through the door. She moved so fast it sounded as though she was breaking in. I jumped out of the way so I wouldn't get knocked over. Her eyes were big and bulgy, and her mouth was open as if frozen mid-sentence. I looked away, pretending nothing was wrong.

'What do you think you're doing?'

She ripped the paper out of my hand and tore it up, right there, in front of me. And then, as if realising what she had done, the expression on her face changed, from anger to shock. I wanted to yell and scream and tell her I just wanted to find out who I was but when I did speak, my voice was calm and soft.

'I'm adopted, aren't I, Mum? Was Gloria Wooding my real name?'

Her shoulders sagged. I felt sorry for upsetting her this way, but I was sorry for myself as well.

'Yes,' she sighed. 'You're adopted.'

She came towards me and put her arm around my shoulder. I wished she would hug me close, or say she loved me. Now I knew I wasn't really hers, maybe that would be too hard.

But she did begin talking to me. She told me that years ago she had lost a baby during pregnancy and hadn't been able to get pregnant again. She and Allan had fostered a baby boy called Terry. His mother didn't want him but she didn't want anyone else to have him either. So they had to take him back to the home when he was nine months old. The last thing Flo heard was Terry crying out for her. I couldn't get this image out of my mind. How hard it must have been for all of them. It wasn't my fault, but I couldn't help feeling guilty and sad, as if it was.

Flo showed me his photo. He was beautiful, with blond curly hair. I didn't know what to say. To cover my confusion, I told her I was going to clean my room, and promised that from now on it would always be tidy. I wanted to show her how grateful I was for being rescued from a life of uncertainty. I wasn't good enough to be kept by my real family. And who knows where I would have ended up if these good people hadn't adopted me.

All the time I was cleaning my room I was thinking about Terry. He looked much more like Flo and Allan than I did. I was brown and didn't look like anyone in the family.

Looking back now, I realise that day I learned what 'feeling grateful' is supposed to be all about.

Chosen

Flo must have phoned her sister Esther, who had just had the phone connected. As soon as I arrived back in Seven Hills, she sat me down in the kitchen, and told me how special I was to have been chosen by Flo and Allan. I sipped a cup of tea while she went on and on but once I was alone the question-and-answer business in my head started up again. I might have been chosen, but was I that special?

I didn't feel special. My real mother probably didn't think I was either, otherwise she would have kept me. There had to be something wrong with me, dating back to when I was born. Even when I was only four years old I'd noticed that my cousins' mantelpieces were full of their baby photos but Flo had no such snaps of me. I'd seen pictures that were taken before I started school, but nothing that said here were these wonderful adopting parents with this specially chosen baby.

That same night, when I had finally fallen asleep, something woke me. I lifted my head off the pillow a little and could feel the end of the mattress rocking up and down. I blinked. There was just enough light coming in the window for me to see that someone was sitting on the end of my bed.

I lay as still as I could. My heart was beating so fast I thought it might jump out of my chest. Had a burglar come through the window? Even as I felt sick with panic I knew that this was unlikely. That window was hard to push up or down and made such a noise everyone in the house would have woken up if someone had tried to get in.

It was a man, but not a stranger. It was Uncle Ernie. He was holding something. Why wasn't Mavis awake and what was her father doing in our room, and on my bed? His and Aunty Esther's room was right next door. I hoped he would think I was asleep. I pulled the sheet tight around me, and tried not to panic. I wanted to see where he was, and what he was doing, but I was too scared to open my eyes. Soon after I heard the shuffling of his slippers on the lino as he left the room.

Things got worse after that. It started one afternoon when I was walking down the side of the house after school. I didn't notice Uncle Ernie until he called out to me. He was at his workbench under the house. In his spare time he made small wooden shadow boxes for displaying ornaments. Aunty had some hanging inside.

They took the bare look off the walls, and sold well up and down the street.

The look on his face made me hesitate. My feet dragged. He stepped out from behind the workbench.

'How do ya like this?' he asked, with a leery smile.

His fly was undone and his thing was hanging out. He went on muttering but I wasn't listening. I turned and ran up the back steps, through the laundry, the kitchen, the lounge room, then down the hall into my room. I slammed the door behind me and stood puffing, pushing my back against the door, shaking. There was no key to lock it, and it wouldn't close properly because he'd done something to the lock.

After a while I stopped shaking and sat on my bed to think. Where was Aunty Esther? Usually I saw her on my way in. Someone was outside. I looked up expecting him, but it was Aunty poking her head in the door. Did I want a cup of tea?

Esther wasn't the kind of person you could talk to—no-one in that house was. There was no-one I could tell about Uncle Ernie's goings on. If I made a point of showing no interest in anything he said or did, he might get the message, and leave me alone. The most important thing was to be on guard all the time, to protect myself.

I tried to concentrate on my schoolwork, but I was tense and wary. I began going to school earlier and earlier, until I was the first there, the first of twelve hundred girls, even in winter. No-one asked why I was first in the gate every day, and one of the last to leave. Mrs Stapleton might have cared though, had she known. She was one of the older teachers, and my favourite. Sure, she growled and was serious, but if you did your homework and showed interest, you'd soon see the funny and kind side as well. She reminded me of Mr McDonald, and she made going to school worthwhile. It would have been good to have had her right through high school.

I was thirteen when I developed a dry cough that kept me awake at night. My aunt insisted I had a cold and refused any suggestion of calling in a doctor. The coughing was so bad I developed tightness in my chest and rib area and was often short of breath. Despite Flo's instructions that Aunty Esther seek medical care, she refused. Instead, she bought pink cough linctus from the chemist because it was cheaper than getting the doctor or taking me to see one.

Soon I began coughing up large amounts of yellow and green sticky phlegm that used to make me dry retch, and sometimes vomit. My legs were trembly. I could hardly walk to the dunny outside. My aunt brought in a plastic bucket, a roll of toilet paper and bits of rag for me to spit and blow my nose into.

'Here, use this and don't get out of bed unless I tell ya to.'

One good thing about being sick was that Uncle Ernie left me alone. I reckon he loathed the very sight of me then. I lay in bed day after day and read Mavis' *True Confession* and *True Romance* books, devouring them one after the other. They had titles like *I denied him—she didn't!* and *Why I married at thirteen and divorced but we couldn't stay apart.*

I think now I probably had a bad dose of bronchitis, or even pneumonia. I was off school for six long weeks. When eventually I went back, Miss McCabe decided I would have to repeat Second Year. I was intent on catching up and in my new class I was soon among the top ten achievers. So pleased were our teachers they began talking about moving some of us into 2DC which was a class or two above. Miss McCabe agreed that five of the ten could be moved but kept the other five back, me among them. Parents came and protested and Miss McCabe had little choice but to move another three students up to join their mates. I had learned not to make a fuss, but was delighted later that year to win prizes—for Art and History, plus another, for being dux of the class.

Uncle Ernie's behaviour took the shine off everything, however. One morning I was in the bathroom getting ready for school. There was no key or lock. Uncle Ernie used to tell everyone that if any of us had an accident no-one would be able to get to them. I knew I was in trouble when the door burst open. Now, suddenly, I realised he'd been planning something like this for a while. His hands were where they shouldn't have been, but I was ready for him. I started swearing, yelling as loudly as I could, scratching, punching. I even spat at him, anything to break free.

But he wouldn't give up, and began hissing, 'C'mon, c'mon. Don't be like that.'

I was both petrified and furious. Petrified that he might overpower me, and angry because he thought he could get away with it. I didn't care if I hurt him. He knew what I thought of him. I'd told him often enough, using the worst possible language when no-one else was around.

It was like being in a boxing ring, little jabs going back and forth. He needed to be in the corner and I needed to be closer to the door to break free. I kept this in mind as we worked our way around the tiny space, being careful not to fall into the bathtub. Finally I was out, running down the hall in my underwear, looking for Aunty Esther. She was in the kitchen. As soon as I saw her I burst into tears. I was trying to tell her what had happened. She turned away and looked out the window.

'Stop tellin' lies,' she screeched, with her back to me.

'I'm not telling lies, it's the truth,' I cried, trying to get through to her. 'God believes me.'

'I'm gonna write to your mother about this and you can read it first, ya hear. Now git to school.'

Cravings

Flo wasn't what you would call a drunk, but more a binge drinker. We didn't keep beer in the house except at Christmas, but once away from home she had a good excuse to down a few. Her headaches had long back become the focus of attention in terms of the way that we did things, but I didn't know if it was the drink that made her headaches worse, or the headaches that drove her to drink.

Arriving home for school holidays, she and Allan would be waiting for me on the platform at Scone, having made the one-hour journey in the boss's Land Rover. Luggage loaded, and we'd be heading for the Willow Tree pub before the train had pulled out of the station.

It was great quenching our thirst in the lounge bar, greeting all the people as they came and went, catching up on gossip. Flo's friendliness and ease, even with strangers, made me proud and resentful at the same time. If only she were interested in her daughter like that. Her headaches were an excuse for not loving me, I thought, for not being present on Speech Day at school where

I was surrounded by everyone else's families but my own. All those parents praising and fussing, that's what I craved for.

It didn't take me long to get bored and after three lemon squashes and trips to the shop to buy aniseed balls, caramels, chocolate freckles, liquorice allsorts and musk sticks, I would be ready to go home. Allan would too. It was he who would have to negotiate the twenty-five miles on a rough country road, most of it unsealed, in the dark. He would then have to get the cows in for milking and put the separator together for the morning.

'C'mon on, Flo,' he'd beg.

'I'll come when I'm good and ready,' she'd reply, raising her voice.

Through a haze of smoke she'd order another round of Resch's—or was it Toohey's?—on tap. I'd stop counting after three. I hated seeing my mother like this and I knew there'd be no tea that night.

That's how it was at the beginning of every holiday. I ate so many lollies during these times that I began having problems with my teeth and boils erupted on my arms and legs.

~

In those last years at Isis River I had to accept that Richard and I were no longer friends. Not after that day he'd hit me on the breast with a tennis ball. It had been his turn to serve at mixed doubles. It wasn't the ball that hurt so much, but his indifference. He didn't acknowledge what had happened, let alone apologise. I was inconsolable.

It was just like Flo said. Once Richard began boarding school and started mixing with rich people, he had no further need with the likes of me. But I did keep thinking about him and remembering the good times we'd had in primary school.

During August when the shearers came in, Richard and I used to visit them after school, and have a cuppa and a jam drop with Cookie on the front steps of the shearing shed, which was less than a hundred yards from school. We didn't know Cookie's real name, we just called him that like everyone else. Our arrival coincided with the shearers' smoko break. Richard and I were always made to feel welcome, providing we behaved ourselves.

One day when Richard was mucking around, Trevor, the wool presser, who looked about seven foot tall, picked Richard up and put him in the press.

'If you don't stop giving cheek, you'll end up in a bale of wool,' said Trevor.

When a couple of tears rolled down Richard's cheeks, I gasped. 'Get him out. Get him out.'

Richard and I stuck up for each other. That's what mates were for, we'd say. But once he started going to that posh boarding school in Sydney, he forgot about me.

I couldn't understand relationships, especially the one Flo

and Allan had with Wally's parents. How could they still be friends when their son had called me a half-caste, four years before? They lived at Snowdon Hall, six miles away. Allan used to borrow the boss's Land Rover so we could go and visit them. Wally was almost fifteen now and very handsome. We sometimes saw each other when we were home on school holidays. He used to board with an older sister in Maitland. I found it hard talking to Wally because I never knew what he was going to say. He both scared and excited me, making me go all goose-bumpy and weak inside. Back at Seven Hills I decided to be brave and write him a love letter.

A few weeks later I was home on holidays and we were visiting Wally's parents. I noticed his mother acting strangely towards me. She had this smile on her face, as if we were sharing some kind of a joke. Then she asked how I was and if I had a boyfriend. I could feel my face getting hot. Oh no, don't tell me! That letter wasn't addressed to her but to Wally. No wonder he didn't say anything.

After that I decided to forget about love for a while and focus more on singing. I sang along with Elvis, Buddy Holly, Paul Anka and the Everley Brothers on the wireless. I fancied myself as a singer. It didn't matter what Mum said, I knew I was good. So good, I would go overseas one day and be discovered, like other talent. I mightn't have made it as a sprinter but singing was another matter.

During these holidays, a friend dropped by to see Mum and Dad, and he brought an unexpected visitor with him, Mr Cutman. It had been five years since I had seen my old adversary and I cautiously walked down the front steps behind Allan to greet him.

Smiling, Mr Cutman moved towards me. We shook hands. He was married now and had extended his teaching contract. He seemed a different person, softer somehow, although his voice still had the same nasal edge. I don't remember what we spoke about, but he was friendly enough.

I wonder now if he ever reflected on his attitude towards me. The best I can say is he had problems with difference. As far as I was concerned, my life was changed by this man. I probably would have left Isis River at the end of primary school anyway because otherwise I would have had to complete high school by correspondence, but I still believe Mr Cutman was the reason Flo and Allan sent me away in my last year. There were two sides to this story, not one. I wish I had been confident enough, brave enough to raise it all with my former teacher that day.

Before those holidays were over, Flo took me to see the dentist in Scone. She had received a letter from my school, raising concerns about the state of my teeth and asking how long it had been since I had visited a dentist. Did Flo know that I had some badly decayed teeth and cavities? Allan was quite embarrassed when, many years later, he told me about this letter.

The dentist removed three teeth, but it was another twelve

months before the rest of the work was done and I was fixed up with a partial denture. I was the ugliest girl at school. There I was with a big gap in my mouth, so glaring I could not be persuaded to smile. Sometimes I would forget, and put my head down as far as I could to avoid eye contact with anyone.

Growing Up

One Saturday morning, just as I was waking up, I heard Aunty speaking with my cousin John in the lounge room. Her voice was raised, as if she wanted me to hear from two rooms away.

'How old do you have to be before you can be charged with defamation of character?'

Shit. What did this mean? I pulled myself up on the pillow, with my ear to the wall, straining to hear John's response. John was my favourite cousin, so what he thought was really important to me. But someone had closed the lounge room door and all I could hear were muffled voices. I seemed to be in big trouble, and could end up in jail or a girls' home. I felt sick to the stomach. What had I done that was so bad to have ended up in this awful place? I couldn't stop shaking.

By the time I got out of bed, Aunty Esther, Uncle Ernie and I were the only ones at home. Mavis had gone away for the weekend, Uncle Ernie was sleeping in the next room after working night shift, and John seemed to have disappeared. Aunty and I didn't speak except to say 'G'morning'. The strained atmosphere between us was palpable and had been building up ever since that morning in the bathroom with Uncle Ernie. Soon after Aunty accosted me in the kitchen.

'Uncle Ernie wants to know why you're not talking to him?'

'You know why,' I replied, not knowing where to look.

It was becoming harder and harder to be in this house, especially because I had no support from anyone. Flo's response when I told her about Ernie wasn't what I expected. I'd been warning her in my letters that I had something to tell her when I arrived home for school holidays. 'What is it?' she kept asking, but I couldn't find the words. What if she didn't believe me?

It wasn't until the very last day of holidays that I plucked up the courage. It was now or never, because I'd run out of time, and my mother needed to know everything. So I blurted it out.

'Ignore him,' she said.

End of conversation. Some things were just relegated to the 'too hard' basket. If we didn't talk about Ernie, then it mustn't have happened. I could only stare at her. I had been manhandled and humiliated by this man day after day for the last three years, and that was all my mother could say.

The following year when I told Allan about Ernie, his reaction took me by surprise. It was too difficult to give him the full story, but there was enough detail for him to get the message.

'I was afraid of what might have been going on, Toots. I know what Ernie's like. He tried showing me his dirty comics and books once. I told him I wasn't interested in that sort of thing. I'm sorry I wasn't able to help.'

Sure, Dad. It was obvious there was no use telling him anything. Even today I wonder about what might have befallen that terrified young girl in the bathroom, ducking and weaving, trying to stay out of Ernie's way, had she not spoken up at all.

Perhaps it was a distraction, a means of survival but in my final years at high school, I became obsessed with the colour of my skin and being different to my family. I was always looking for people like me. My best friend Anne was one of these people.

Anne had short, curly dark hair, brown eyes, an olive complexion and a smile that lit up her face and made heads turn. I thought she was beautiful. On cloudy days, my hair went curly too. Allan used to say that's how he knew it was going to rain. But Anne didn't resemble her parents in any way; they were white like mine, and it was obvious she wasn't. And her brother looked old enough to be her father. Maybe Anne and I were related. Was it possible to find out without asking?

Asking anything about anything in those days seemed to get me in all sorts of trouble. Flo threatened time and again to send me to Parramatta Girls' Home if I misbehaved or didn't stop asking 'bloody' questions. She made that home sound like a jail. It looked like it too, from a distance, when I saw that building many years later, rearing in its ugliness above the surrounding wall like a beast in search of prey.

Anne and her family lived in a Housing Commission settlement at Riverwood, which had once been army barracks. Their home was one of many small dwellings connected by a series of wooden ramps. Unlike me, Anne wasn't searching for answers. I don't think she knew she was adopted. That was the big difference between her and me. She was happy and I was miserable.

Each time Anne invited me to stay at her place for the weekend I would answer 'yes' before she had even finished asking. Going to Anne's meant being fussed over and answering lots of questions. Anne's parents were strict with her, yet interested and kind to her friends. It was a different story when it came to Anne staying with me. A visit to Waverley Station went well but the tension in the air at Seven Hills meant I never invited her again.

How I longed to be like Anne, to really belong in a family, even though I could see that there were restrictions placed on her. I was the only friend Anne was allowed out with. Sometimes I felt like her babysitter, although she was a couple of months older than me. Flo said I should have been flattered but I wasn't really—I wanted someone to look after me for a change.

Finally, the big day arrived. I had passed the Intermediate Certificate, graduated as dux of the class, and could leave school. Hip, hip, hooray. No more prefects. No more last warnings. Excitement filled the air. I was free of high school—free of rigid rules. Never again would I have to wear that ridiculous winter uniform. I would be hatless, gloveless and stockingless from now on and evermore. Flo was forever saying her school days were the best days of her life and that I would be sorry now mine were over.

I was one of the first out the gate.

A New Place

Miss McCabe had written me such a glowing school report I was sure it was meant for someone else. But no, there was my name on it. Maybe she wasn't so bad after all. But hang on, I couldn't let her off that easily, and still can't, not even today, fifty years later.

Writing this now, I am again that twelve-year-old girl in the quadrangle. It is the price I—and plenty of others—paid, and still pay, for being poor. That morning line-up ordeal at assembly, being singled out for something that was really minor or petty, feeling crushed and humiliated, has shaped the woman I have become and I cannot agree with those who say, 'But that's how it was in our day. It was for our own good.' Own good, be damned!

So there I was, school years already disappearing into the past, the world was my oyster. I could do what I liked, especially as Flo had yet to make the move from Isis River. Her irritation echoed down the line.

'Why work in a factory when you got good marks for typing and bookkeeping, and passed your Intermediate Certificate?'

I wanted to tell her that my experience at school was enough to turn me off typing for life. I simply didn't want to be reminded of it in any way. Whitmont's, the shirt people, had a vacancy going for a junior process worker, machining shirt cuffs. I liked sewing, and needed a job pronto, in order to buy clothes for myself.

I was soon to learn that industrial sewing machines were a lot different to the domestic variety. Not only were they bigger, heavier, faster and noisier, they were downright dangerous. More like monsters than machines, they needed to be approached with caution. But knowing this was one thing, putting that caution into practice day after day, was something else.

Production was paramount at Whitmont's. Each machinist had to sew a quota, or part thereof, each day. Once you got past that magic number you could earn a bonus, which meant more money in your pocket. Those first few days the foreman hung around, adjusting and attaching metal plates and screws to make the machine go faster, so I could earn a good bonus. He demonstrated various tasks again and again and then, finally, it was my turn. I must have picked things up quickly because he seemed impressed and a little while later he left me with a pile of cuffs.

I pressed my foot hard on the pedal. I was so enthusiastic I forgot to check where my fingers were—until I heard the crunch. The needle had run through my middle finger and snapped in two. It took some moments for me to feel the pain. I don't remember who pressed the buzzer, but assistance was immediate.

'It might be an idea to lie down,' said the nurse, reaching for a pair of pliers.

I had been working at Whitmont's for nine months when Flo and Allan moved to Sydney. They stayed with Aunty Esther and Uncle Ernie until they could find a place of their own. I liked to think that it had been my letters to them over the years that did the trick, but probably the real reason was that Flo had had enough of the bush and needed to be closer to specialist care for her headaches.

My mother's decision to leave Waverley Station only six months before my father was due for his ten-year long service leave, however, left them with little money for a fresh start. When Allan tried to discuss the subject, Flo did her block. When Flo wanted to do something, she went ahead with it, no matter the cost or inconvenience. One day I asked her why she couldn't have waited another six months.

'Don't you start,' she said. 'Your father's bad enough.'

At sixteen years of age I still didn't know how my adoptive parents really felt about me. Allan was a demonstrative man most of the time, and because he showed me affection, I felt there was something strong between us. Whereas since Flo was always telling me what I should and shouldn't be doing, I'd long understood how unpredictable she could be. I had learned to question how much of my parents' love I could take for granted. Not once in that five-year period had either of them ever made the effort to attend any of my school functions. At least they didn't forget my birthday, because it fell a few days into the New Year, during school holidays. And of course, I was there to remind them.

Children of my generation were expected to get on with life, tough it out, accept whatever circumstances their parents chose for them, but by comparison other parent-child relationships seemed much more loving and considerate. And that difference between what I could see around me and what I was experiencing added to my doubts. I was like a child on a merry-go-round, coming back again and again to the same place and the same question. Why did Flo and Allan adopt me?

After living with Aunty Esther and Uncle Ernie for two months, Allan had had enough. He was adamant. Flo was to take the first place she could find because he couldn't stand living with her relatives any longer. I wondered what he would have been like after five and a half years.

In November 1959, we moved into a three-roomed fibro garage in Blacktown. It wasn't much of a place, but it was ours, and we were free to do as we pleased without being answerable to Esther all the time. Rent was five pounds a week. I slept in the kitchen. In the daytime my chrome bed was the lounge. Living with my parents meant safety, but there were rules, so many rules I wasn't used to. Flo expected me home at a certain time, and then wanted to know where I was going and who I was going with. She knew I smoked, like her and Allan, but she didn't want me drinking. I didn't tell her that I already was, because it was only on Fridays, after work, with Mavis.

'There'll be plenty of time for drinking,' said Flo. 'You don't have to do what I do.'

She was always saying that.

It was hard to work out what was expected of me. More like trying to read Flo's mind. I felt sure if I stayed at my friend Violet's place overnight it would be okay. Vi was the third youngest of ten living children, six of them still at home, so there were always people coming and going. I loved being a part of this large noisy family. Vi told me I was mad, and that she'd trade places with me any time. We never tired of being in each other's company, even after working together all day. We'd been having such a good time, talking and listening to music.

'Why don't you stay the night?' she asked.

So I did. I'd told Flo where I was going before I left home. But when I walked in the door next morning, I realised I should have phoned and left a message with our landlady.

'Don't ever do that to me again, Lorraine. I thought something must have happened to you.'

I'd never seen her look like this before. I tried to be positive. Maybe all these rules meant she cared after all.

I was seventeen when Flo's brain tumour was diagnosed by Dr Khrivanek at our local surgery. My mother didn't like foreigners, unless they spoke the kind of English she could understand. In shops, if they got in her way with their trolleys she would kick them—and I do mean kick them.

'Speak English,' she'd say.

How much of her erratic behaviour was caused by the pituitary tumour and how much was in her personality is hard, even now, to know. But Dr Khrivanek realised right away what the problem was. He'd seen it before, so he knew what he was talking about.

My mother had acromegaly, a characteristic sign of a pituitary tumour. A broad nose, lantern jaw, spade-like hands and broad feet. Overactivity of the growth hormone in her pituitary gland caused this bony overgrowth, resulting in ring and shoe-width changes to accommodate the expansion. Her headaches were a classic sign. The doctor asked to see photos of Flo from years ago and pointed out her once-fine facial features compared to how they were now. She had indeed changed dramatically in the last ten years and this seemed to coincide with the onset of her headaches.

Dr Khrivanek opened one of his medical books and showed Flo a picture of someone with the same disease as her. He ordered tests and x-rays to confirm his diagnosis. He said an operation was considered too risky to the optic nerve. So Flo began medication and was to be assessed later.

Following the diagnosis my mother was advised not to drink. She abstained for a week, then went back to her old habits. Sometimes she'd drink on an empty stomach, which made her vomit. I tried to discourage her because I was the one who had to clean up.

She used to drink with her mates at the Robin Hood Hotel, opposite Blacktown Railway Station. That's where she had met Mrs Janes, Vi's mother. Vi and I were still inseparable, and it wasn't long before she introduced me to her older brother, Jimmy.

Buckwheat

Jimmy was wearing tight, white 'footie' shorts the day we met. He was a football star, with a black crew cut, and so handsome. He looked like Warren Williams, a popular rock'n'roll singer. Jimmy reckoned he signed Warren William's autograph to unsuspecting fans, but we couldn't be sure because he was always clowning around. He was two years older than me, and acted tough, so I played hard to get, to show I wasn't easy. According to Flo, too many girls were. They went out with the first person who asked them, and had sex if that was on the menu. Shotgun weddings were not unusual. It was either get married or give your baby up for adoption, if your family weren't supportive. There was a new pill that people were talking about; it was supposed to stop girls from getting pregnant, but no-one seemed to know anything more than that. The fella, of course, could always use a condom.

It wasn't long before Jimmy's mother, his mates and sisters started pushing us together. Allan said Mrs Janes was after a daughter-in-law, not that I would have minded, but I thought eighteen was too young to be tied down with one bloke for the rest of my life. It was about then, or a bit later, that I noticed Jimmy's mates calling him 'bunger'. A bunger is a firecracker and they said it was because he went off with a bang. They'd fall about laughing and I pretended I understood and laughed with them.

Vi said to be careful of Jimmy because he had once rejected one of her friends. I began to worry. If he found out I was adopted, he might drop me, and being dropped by Jimmy was the worst thing I could possibly imagine. So I let him think I wasn't interested, even when thoughts of him filled my every waking moment.

Every Saturday afternoon Jimmy and his mates watched this show on television called *Our Gang*. They used to roll around on the lounge or floor, clutching their sides and roaring with laughter. I thought it was a kids' program. It seemed to be about a group of young American boys and the mischief they got up to with billycarts, and about boys being boys. One little fella in the gang was Afro-American; his name was Buckwheat. I thought he was cute, but I didn't say anything because Jimmy didn't need any prompting to tease me.

Before long, he started calling me Buckwheat. Then his mates got in on the act.

'I'm not black,' I told them. 'Leave me alone.'

The more I reacted the worse they got, and I would be on the verge of tears.

'How can I make them stop?' I asked Jimmy's sister, Joyce.

'Ignore them,' she said.

So, I did. Joyce was right. Jimmy stopped, but his mates kept it up, until he stepped in.

'Stop it. Her name's Lorraine.'

And Lorraine it was, ever after. The change was amazing. They'd had their share of fun at my expense, and now wanted to make up. From then on I was treated like royalty. It was weird. Jimmy made no attempt to hide his feelings and kept asking me out. His love was in his eyes, his voice, his touch—not that we ever did anything but kiss.

One day I asked Flo what she would do if I got pregnant. Perhaps I was testing her love but I also wanted to be prepared should it happen. She said she would kick me out, that's what. She also said that she didn't want people knowing I was adopted either. I couldn't understand this at all. Was it because she hadn't come to terms with her infertility and felt guilty because of it? Was adoption meant to be a secret? Why couldn't I talk about it? Would my real mother, wherever she was, whoever she was, want to keep me a secret too? I didn't like hassling Flo, about this or anything, because it just made her angry. Besides, I reckoned she'd been through enough, what with a miscarriage, not being able to conceive again, having to leave Terry in a home, hearing him cry, adopting me who must have been a disappointment because I didn't look like anyone else in the family, and then being diagnosed with a brain tumour. Flo had enough to contend with.

Adding to my layers of confusion were the scraps of information Flo fed me about my biological mother. She told me of a day when my birth mother had come to our home in Marrickville when I was a toddler.

'She doesn't recognise me,' said the young woman to Flo.

'Would you recognise someone you hadn't seen since you were a baby?' responded Flo.

Flo told me that the young woman was beautiful and that she was about nineteen years old. Apparently Flo went to the police station afterwards and put a restraining order on her so she wouldn't be allowed to come near us again.

Later, when I asked Allan what he knew about this, he said that Flo had told him the same story and that she was very agitated at the time.

'Mum had no reason to lie, Toots.'

So being adopted not only meant being grateful for the rest of my life, it also meant not ever talking about it to anyone. There were times I wanted to lash out, not with my fists but my words. It was so frustrating, pretending I belonged to people who I had nothing in common with, when my real family was out there somewhere. All I wanted was to be like my friends and to know who I was.

One day something inside me rebelled and I told a woman at work that I had two brothers and a sister. My cousin Mavis, who was working with me at Whitmont's, later told her that I was an only child. You could say I was lying but I knew in my heart, in my very bones, that I had siblings somewhere. Nonetheless, I did feel guilty whenever that woman looked at me after that. We didn't speak again.

Towards the end of 1960 I left Whitmont's for a job as a shop assistant in Winn's Department Store. I was sent to work in the dress materials department. I loved my job, but I had yet to work out what to do about Jimmy. He took to calling in to see me at work. One day when I saw him coming, I ran and hid behind a rack of clothes in the children's department.

I heard him calling my name, but stayed put. I wanted to tell him how much he meant to me, but in panic about my origins, I kept running away. I was convinced he deserved someone better than me. But I was holding off hurt too. My reasoning was that no-one could love me for long. When Jimmy understood, really understood my background, he'd be the one doing the running.

But his mother acted as if I could do no wrong. She was always singing my praises. It was embarrassing. I liked her a lot, but her voice was so loud, she would have made a good town crier. One night, when Jimmy, his family and mates were gathered in the lounge room watching *Bandstand* on the television, Mrs Janes took the floor and stunned the gathering with her announcement.

'Jimmy has got himself a little black girl.'

The silence that followed was awful, but I wasn't game to look around. I slunk out of the room before anyone could put me on the spot with questions I couldn't answer.

It's both strange and sad when I think about it now. Vi was my best friend, yet I never once discussed Jimmy and how I felt about him with her. Jimmy and I dated only three times in the next year or so, but whenever he saw me around, he'd still ask me out. But I was running too fast to appreciate how hard he tried to reach me, to be with me.

~

My next job was with the Postmaster General's Department, known by everyone as the PMG. I was employed as a telephonist, doing shift-work in the city, in Martin Place. PMG-trained telephonists were highly sought after by employment agencies. The training was from four to six weeks, and every few months monitors 'upstairs' would listen in to see if we were performing our job properly. There were certain procedures and protocols to follow. After all, we were a part of the Public Service, and that's what we were expected to provide.

Flo seemed happier. She felt I was climbing the ladder of respectability. I was nineteen now, and our relationship had moved into calmer waters. It was nice not being at loggerheads with each other all the time. I have no idea what contributed to this change, whether it was Flo's new medication, me becoming an adult and not asking so many questions, or both of these things. I only knew she was fun to be around and to go shopping with.

It was a good time for us, with Flo, Nanna and I making the occasional train trip down the South Coast to Figtree to visit Nanna's relatives. We still had disagreements, but nothing like before, and mercifully this relative harmony lasted on and off for the next three years.

The following year, I was staying with a friend, Judy Thelan, near Wollongong. As soon as I woke up, I knew something had happened to me, but I didn't know what because I kept drifting off. My chest felt tender and when I took a deep breath it hurt. It was as if someone very heavy had been walking on my chest.

'Has this happened to you before?' asked a blurry figure in white.

Had what happened? Where was I? And who was this man? When I regained consciousness, my ulcerated tongue made it difficult to speak.

'The doctor says you have had a grand mal epileptic fit,' said Mrs Thelan, holding my hand in hers.

She made me some broth, and looked after me as if I were one of her own. She was the mother of ten, and a warmer and more loving woman you wouldn't meet.

'What were you two kids up to last night?' she asked.

I didn't tell her that Judy and I were out boozing, and that I was trying to get away from some bloke I wasn't interested in.

My body was going haywire and I had no idea what was going on. There had already been two or three recent incidents when I had tripped and fallen down stairs, at home and at work. I hurt my knee after a fall at home and I don't know whether it was to do with the antibiotics I was prescribed, but my joints began to swell. First my knee, then my ankle and soon after my elbow, which I couldn't straighten and had to wear in a sling.

I lost count of the doctors and specialists I was referred to. Three doctors asked if I'd had rheumatic fever as a child.

'No,' said Flo.

They enquired about the family history. Flo was adamant that no-one else in our family had ever had epilepsy. I can't explain why I didn't intervene but although my medical history was my own, I held back from telling the doctors that I was adopted. Flo had made it clear that this was a matter not to be discussed.

All the medical tests were inconclusive. I was prescribed medication for epilepsy, but it didn't stop my imagination getting the better of me. I was terrified I would have a seizure on the way to work, and would wake up to find strangers standing around and gawking down at me.

So not only had I had an epileptic seizure—the first of five over the next four years—but my life had become one big lie. Now, there were two things I needed to keep to myself. Adoption and epilepsy.

I wanted to ask Flo about my biological parents but there seemed little point in creating a fuss over something that would only aggravate her and make her more determined not to tell me anything. I knew how stubborn she could be.

Sometimes I would tease her, hoping she would become so exasperated that she would blurt something out, but it didn't work. She would just throw something at me, anything she could get her hands on.

I was in the Robin Hood Hotel celebrating my twenty-first birthday with Flo and her friends, when two of Jimmy's mates came over to tell me that Jimmy had just got engaged. I put on a brave face but my legs were shaking. I felt so weak I thought I might faint. The next time I saw him, months later, he asked me out.

'But you're a married man now, Jimmy,' I protested.

'That's your fault,' he replied.

For many years I would continue to think about what he said and wonder how my life might have panned out had I done things differently.

Mistaken for a Maori

In 1965, Flo's health took a turn for the worse and her short-term memory became a problem. The doctors advised she be put into care, but Allan would have no part of it. He couldn't—wouldn't—abandon her. A month in Royal North Shore Hospital and various tests later she came home. Her comments had Allan and me worried. She said she was waiting for him to come home from the homestead, and that she had better set the table. It was six years since they'd left Waverley. And Allan was already in the kitchen. The two of us looked at each other.

Allan and I now had two jobs each. One we got paid for, the other was looking after Flo. She was a difficult patient. My bosses were accommodating, arranging my shifts so that Flo was on her own for as little time as possible. But I didn't know if I was coming or going. I had another seizure, followed by another just a couple of weeks later.

Both times I was at home and my friend Barbara was with me. After I'd regained consciousness, Barbara said, 'Don't ever think you're mother doesn't love you, Lorraine, because she does. I had two patients while you were unconscious on the floor. Your mother was yelling out. She was crying, "Do something. Do something for my Lorraine." '

I was surprised, yet happy to hear this.

The doctors advised me to get away, to take a holiday from all the responsibility. Allan and I agreed. It was time to take that working holiday in New Zealand, the one I'd been thinking about for a while.

It was shortly after my twenty-third birthday that I set sail. Carol, a friend from work, was travelling with me. We spent six weeks in Auckland and then it was time to head south in search of fruit-picking. We were joined by Jenny, who also worked at the GPO, but two was company and three a crowd in our poky caravan with too much luggage, no car and a moody room-mate.

However all that seemed trivial compared to my worries about home. Since I'd been away, Allan and Flo had moved from Blacktown to a Housing Commission flat in Redfern. I wondered how Allan was coping and whether I should return to Australia.

The girls in the packing shed, all Maoris except one, made time pass quickly with their friendship and laughter. We'd meet each evening, share stories, and watch television in the tin hut that served as our lounge room.

Our elderly boss, a widower, shared an adjoining orchard with his son and family. He would call for us each morning in his ancient, red, well-maintained Mercedes. He enjoyed young company and was hopeful we might stay on, but twelve weeks was long enough. We headed further south.

Christchurch in May can be freezing, as it was in 1966. Accommodation was tight that year as well. But after some door knocking we were successful. A men's boarding house. We didn't mind, if she didn't, we told our elderly landlady.

Settled and soon employed at Aulsebrook's chocolate and biscuit factory, our social life was soon on the up and up. We found ourselves more and more attracted to Maoris and their parties. We reckoned their parties were better than Pakehas' anytime. They didn't need record players or stereograms. They'd just pick up their guitars and start singing and dancing. And I'd sing and dance along with them.

One afternoon a carload of Maoris pulled up outside our boarding house. Thinking they were the same fellas from the army barracks we'd met the previous night, I walked over to talk to them. The driver greeted me like a long-lost friend, but I'd never seen him before.

'He's speaking to you,' whispered Carol.

'Well I don't know what he's saying, do I? I'm not Maori.'

I told him and his mates that I was Australian, but he kept shaking his head, as if he didn't believe me, so I walked away.

All too soon I was back home. It seemed I'd never been away. Getting Flo bathed and dressed was a battle in itself. She fought

Allan and me as though her life depended on it and perhaps for her, in her deteriorating state of mind, it did.

I began going out at night with my best friend Barbara, drinking more and more and smoking too. And that's how I lived my life, working, coming home, caring for Flo, then taking every free moment to numb myself with grog and fags. I counted the days to my next holiday.

In July 1967, I set out on a Redline tour to Central Australia and Darwin, via Brisbane. Twenty-one glorious days of freedom, I could hardly contain my excitement.

It seemed inevitable that Jack and I would get together. We were strangers travelling on a coach full of oldies. Assuming he was from Sydney, I remarked how good it was to get away.

'Wouldn't know,' he replied, in an English accent I found hard to place. 'Only been in the country a week.'

Jack's plan was to leave the coach in Brisbane the following morning and look for a job as a radio operator. I wanted to ask why Brisbane and not Sydney, but there'd be no point. We wouldn't be seeing each other again.

Soon, thoughts of Jack and Brisbane were far behind me. I had teamed up with Frank, a publican in his fifties and Pat, a bank-teller in her late thirties. We shared meals and would congregate at the bar each night to debrief at the end of another long, dusty day. The distances were vast. 'Six thousand miles in twenty-one days,' the brochure said.

An unlikely group, we attracted attention wherever we went. We met so many people, embellishing each other's stories with every round of drinks. I hadn't expected to come across so many unattached males, but welcomed the attention.

Our first night in Alice Springs, we attended a corroboree. I wanted to see more, to ask questions, but everyone got up and left straight after the performance. To me that didn't seem right, but I didn't know why.

Shortly afterwards two young men approached. One was white and spoke with an English accent; the other was olive brown, like me, with a smile that was hard to resist.

'I'm Aboriginal,' he said, introducing himself and his mate.

I nodded and smiled. 'I'm Australian.'

I admired the way he knew exactly who he was. I didn't have a clue who my real self was. It was as if I had just appeared out of the blue, alone, lacking even luggage.

It was cold, dark, wet and windy when, a few weeks later, the coach pulled into the Sydney terminal. Allan was waiting. We greeted and hugged each other.

'Toots, there's someone waiting to see you. A young fella.'

'Who is it, Dad?'

'I don't know. Never seen him before. He says you met in Brisbane. This is him now. Says his name's Jack.'

Throwback

Flo kept asking the same question over and over again, her voice rising, then dropping as she said my name.

'What's the matter, Lorraine? What's the matter?'

Allan spoke like a man with a mission.

'You'll have to tell Jack,' he said, sliding the phone across the table towards me.

It was March 1968, and I had only just accepted Jack's proposal of marriage. Now I felt like a deflated balloon. All the air had gone out of me. I didn't understand what my father was saying.

It had been eight months since Jack and I had met on the coach to Brisbane and we'd been instantly smitten. But I hadn't expected to see him again, let alone have him waiting for me at the coach terminal when I had arrived back in Sydney. He let on only a few days after our reunion that he had a job lined up in Mt Isa, working in the mines. He needed the money, he said, but I hadn't wanted to hear any more. I was just getting to know and care about this bloke and now he was going out of my life again.

'I'm leaving next week,' he told me.

Did he expect me to wait for him? He seemed all over the place. When his first letter from Mt Isa arrived, I remember taking a deep breath. He said he was already half in love with me. But he was up there and I was down here. Besides, I'd never heard of anyone being half in love.

'A lot can happen before we see each other again,' I wrote.

'I know. That's why I don't propose to leave it for long.'

When Jack arrived back in Sydney on Boxing Day 1967, he'd been up at Mt Isa for four and a half months. He asked me to go with him to South Africa to live.

'South Africa? Apartheid? No thanks.'

My complexion was deep olive, like a good suntan, and although Jack said he had no problems with my colour, I had qualms. I was rattled by him asking me to go to South Africa with him. And even more shocked when he told me that in his opinion apartheid worked.

Several weeks later Jack popped the question. I saw him as a sophisticated man of the world. Born in Dorset, England, he had lived in South Africa and Rhodesia, been a Congo mercenary, and spoke three languages. But when he proposed marriage, at first I didn't respond.

'I'm not going to a country that treats people like that. No way.'

That's when he asked for my hand again, only this time on bended knee. I hesitated. Jack had given me a lot to think about. After giving in and ruling South Africa out as a place to live, he then wanted to know whether I would wait while he went and fought the civil war that was taking place in Angola. He'd fought as a mercenary in the Congo less than a year before, and told me that he hadn't known whether he'd come out of it alive or not.

I shook my head in exasperation. Was I really up to sharing my life with this all-over-the-place, risk-taking, adventure-seeking romantic? There was only one way to find out. So when he proposed this second time I accepted graciously, hoping it was the right thing to do. I had never seen a man so besotted. Even my workmates had commented on it, having seen us together one day after work.

After Allan told me about my Negro father, I felt sure Jack wouldn't want to marry me, not after he learned that I was coloured. No-one would, and you couldn't blame them. I should have known better. It had all been too good to be true, this idea of *me* getting married. The way I figured it, each time Jack made love to me, he'd be wondering if he was with a white woman or a black one.

My father was insistent that I call Jack, so I dialled his number. I knew it off by heart. He answered promptly.

'What's the matter, sweetheart?'

'Can you come over? Dad said I have to tell you something. It's important.'

When the doorbell rang, Allan ushered Jack in and patted the seat opposite. Flo just sat there, not saying anything. Jack looked around the room and I could tell by the creases on his forehead that he was worried. But soon our relationship would be over and, in time, he would meet someone else. Someone who didn't have Negro blood in them, or who brought the worry of giving birth to a 'throwback' baby.

I struggled on but I was crying so much I was almost incoherent. And I couldn't work out why Jack didn't bugger off while he had the opportunity. Clearly he wasn't listening to anything I was saying. I looked at him smiling and frowning. Did he think this was funny?

I looked down at the rug at my feet. Allan took over and delivered his information like a minister giving a sermon in church. I listened while he and Jack talked about me as if Flo and I were no longer in the room. They were discussing where Jack and I should go to be alone, to talk. About what, I didn't know.

On our way down the hall to catch the lift, Jack begged me to look at him. But I couldn't. I was too ashamed. Why didn't he just leave me alone and stop trying to dry my tears? Couldn't he see that nothing would ever be the same again, no matter how much he wanted to make love to me, to prove how much he cared? He thought making love was the answer to everything. 'Make love, not war' was his mantra.

'Sweetheart, you don't look like a Negro,' he was keen to reassure me. 'Your features are too fine. Believe me, I know. I've travelled a lot and lived in Africa, remember?'

Minutes later, although it felt like hours, we caught a bus to the Adams Hotel in the city. Jack ordered a beer but I don't remember what I drank. I only remember the thick pile cushions in the hotel lounge, and their mushroomy, velvety texture.

Jack wouldn't take no for an answer. He was intent on us getting married straightaway. He wanted to get me away from home, he said, away from responsibility for my mother's health, as far from Sydney as he could manage. He was now suggesting one of three places. Mt Tom Price in Western Australia, Mt Morgan in Queensland, or Papua New Guinea. The choice was mine, he said.

Then and there, I chose Papua New Guinea. It sounded exotic, and appealed to my sense of adventure. But mostly I just sat there in the pub that evening, staring straight ahead. I couldn't trust myself to say what I was really thinking. I was remembering how strongly I had felt when I was younger about wanting to find my birth family. It was Flo's photo album that had started the ball rolling. My feelings about the colour of my skin had been intense back then, even though getting Flo to admit I was adopted had been a struggle. Oddly enough, this intensity receded as I'd passed from teenage years to early adulthood. Perhaps I thought that I no longer stood out quite as much, although I was still frequently asked if I was Italian or Greek and, on that holiday in New Zealand, I was even taken to be a Maori.

But now, faced with this new information about my Negro father, it seemed to me that marriage to Jack was not such a good idea. Living with white parents, growing up in a white society, I had internalised prejudiced negativity about dark skin. I was both an insider and an outsider. I had already felt the rejection that came simply because of my skin colour but, despite what I came to believe years later was racism, I was still trying to fit in. It was like my body was experiencing the distress, the anguish, but my head was still looking at the world from my white adoptive parents' point of view. I was alarmed at what I might find if I started looking for this unknown father, a man without a name. It was him who had coloured my life; he had caused this heartache, not my white mother. Trying to fit in meant trying to be white, and a nameless Negro father was a shameful thing.

I finally understood that I had one foot in Australia and the other somewhere over there, in America. The joke was on me, but I wasn't laughing. I looked at Jack. Whatever happened, it was too painful to go through a night like this again with anyone else.

~

The following day my eyelids were so puffed up I had difficulty opening them. When the girls at work asked if I was all right, I just told them that my eyes were sore and left it at that. I was twenty-five years of age, but seemed to have aged overnight. As far as I was concerned there was nothing to look forward to anymore. But Jack saw things differently and wouldn't be deterred. In spite of everything he'd been told of my background, and my constant teariness, his plan was for us to marry the next week and leave Sydney the week after that. He'd made enquiries with the registry office, and their requirements and dates fitted in with his plans.

For me, there were too many things happening. I couldn't keep up. I should have seen it coming, but maybe I didn't want to until Jack had proposed. How could I get married and leave Sydney? Who would look after Flo? Allan couldn't do it on his own. Jack would have to go to Papua New Guinea without me. Besides, I told him, it would give him more time to think about us and what he was letting himself in for. I didn't want him marrying in haste and regretting it later on.

Jack left for Port Moresby a week later. Before he flew out, he insisted I set a wedding date. I could see he loved me, but I didn't want him to because I wasn't entirely sure if I felt the same about him. He didn't seem to understand that I was responsible for Flo's welfare. I felt numb, as if what was happening wasn't real. A future with me looked very bleak. I was barely holding together, but finally decided that if I didn't go along with his plans, I might fall apart completely, and I couldn't afford that. So, I circled the fifteenth of June—it meant twelve weeks of separation that Jack wasn't happy about, but it didn't stop him going. He said he'd write twice a week, and made me promise to do the same. It didn't matter if our letters overlapped.

'Just keep writing,' he said.

The social worker at Royal Prince Alfred Hospital kept reassuring me that Flo would be well looked after in the Rozelle Admission Centre, as she called it, but I really knew it was Rozelle Psychiatric Hospital.

'And now you are getting married,' she said, 'and really, there is nothing more the doctors can do...'

In 1965, after Flo had spent a month at Royal North Shore Hospital, Allan was told he needed to make a decision about her future care. We'd never be able to manage at home, the specialist told him. But Allan couldn't abandon Flo, so he had brought her home and we'd been looking after her in her deteriorating state. It would have cost a lot to put her where the specialist suggested. Allan didn't say where the place was, he just said he didn't have enough money.

Before her diagnosis, my mother had run up debts that my father hadn't known about. She had a long history of buying things on hire purchase, shouting rounds of drinks at the pub, and helping her sister Esther out. Flo was generous to a fault. Years later, Allan's wages were still garnisheed. In view of these financial circumstances the social worker advised that Flo be admitted to Rozelle. We kept arguing that Flo wasn't mad, she had a brain tumour, but in the end things could not continue as they'd been. We were desperate and the hospital was free.

To add to my worries, I had more tests to determine the cause of my epilepsy but they too were inconclusive. It was thought I had too much responsibility at home. Although Allan was concerned about my health, I didn't tell him or the doctors that I was drinking too much, binge drinking mostly, and had taken to cigarettes with a vengeance. As far as I was concerned, the booze and fags were the only tools I had to help me cope.

Miscommunication

Jack's telegram arrived in June 1968, some three months after his departure. What was he up to now, I wondered as I tore the envelope open. All he said was, 'Moving from Mendi. Be in touch soon. Trust me. Love Jack.' He didn't say where he was going or why. Maybe he had met someone else. In a way I was wishing he had. He was twenty-nine, good-looking and alone up there. I would have been disappointed but not surprised, if he'd strayed. It would have explained his sudden move from Mendi near Mt Hagen in the Southern Highlands.

It would be another four weeks before I heard from him again. Up until this time his expressions of love and longing had been arriving in the mail twice-weekly, regular as clockwork, then nothing. Our proposed June wedding date had come and gone. He phoned from Port Moresby twice during that time, but each time I wasn't home, and he refused to leave any messages with Allan. I was so worked up by now that I decided to place an advertisement in the *South Pacific Post*, a newspaper produced in Port Moresby. I also wrote a letter to his old address in Mendi saying that I now realised he wouldn't go ahead with the marriage. I wrote other stuff as well—I was heartbroken.

My ad was simple, and straightforward. 'If anyone knows the whereabouts of Jack Cowell, could they please ask him to phone his fiancée, Lorraine, in Sydney.' I included my phone number.

In hindsight, it was probably the worst thing I could have done, but how else was I to contact this elusive man? Jack needed to know how much his lack of communication had impacted on me. Allan thought my actions too hasty, but I was beyond reasoning by then. Just six weeks earlier Jack had sent a cheque, asking me to buy both an engagement and wedding ring.

'Get something nice, something you like,' he wrote.

I was already wearing the engagement ring.

I felt like a mouse on a wheel, running, running, trying to catch up. Eventually Jack got in touch but he didn't explain where he'd been during those four weeks. He made the arrangements for me to join him in Port Moresby but by then I was more distressed and angry than excited at the thought of seeing him again.

My distress and anger were complicated by the conflicting feelings I had for dumping Flo in Rozelle. Although I was relieved, I knew Flo wasn't being looked after like she was at home and I felt guilty.

When Jack phoned to let us know that he was working at Boroko Motors as a used car salesman, Allan pleaded with me to join him in Port Moresby. Jack had always spoken highly of Allan, saying that he would hate to be on the wrong side of him, and so I asked Allan to speak to Jack man-to-man and find out what was going on. But it was not to be.

'He's not a man's bootlace as far as I'm concerned,' said my father, throwing the receiver at me. 'I don't want to talk to him, not after what he's done to you. Just go to Port Moresby, Toots, and work it out. It'll be easier when the two of you are together.'

I was confused. One minute he was saying Jack's not a man's bootlace, and the next telling me to join him. I expected Allan to call Jack a bastard, because that's what I wanted to call him, but I had no fight left in me. Allan was living in fairyland if he thought Jack and I could work it out on our own. This was the first time I'd asked him to do anything. I couldn't believe he'd let me down.

It was a cold August morning when I flew out of Sydney. I tried to think positively, but my head was overflowing with thoughts and questions. It was a long five-hour flight.

Where was he, I wondered, looking around, as I stepped onto the tarmac in steamy Moresby, pantyhose and nylon petticoat clinging to my skin under the gabardine dress. It was obvious I was overdressed for the tropics; I was the only one carrying an overcoat and wearing stockings.

Surely this wasn't him coming towards me. The closer he got, the more I wanted to run. His face was tight and hard, as if he were trying to hold himself together. Yet I had more reason to be angry than he did. Maybe Flo was right when she said I was a fool for running after him. But it was too late to turn back now.

After saying hullo and kissing me on the cheek, he remarked that my hair was too short.

'You look like a lesbian, except I know you're not.'

I was too stunned to reply. All I could do was to look at the ground and feel even more ashamed and inferior.

'We should have got married and come up here together, like I wanted you to, remember? I needed a steadying influence. Why didn't you come with me, Lorraine?'

Was this about my haircut, or had he done something he shouldn't have and needed a scapegoat? Not once did he apologise, explain himself or ask how my mother was. I realised then I was stuck with a man I no longer recognised.

On the way to the hotel, Jack went on and on about the ad I'd put in the paper. I looked out the car window, still none the wiser as to where he'd disappeared to during those four weeks.

The following week I received a telegram at the telephone exchange in Moresby where I worked. It was from Allan. Flo had been found unconscious on the floor of the ward at the hospital. I rang home immediately.

'Don't come. Stay where you are. There's nothing you can do, Toots.'

A few weeks later, the second telegram arrived. My mother was dead.

There was only one service a day out of Moresby, but by the time I could arrange a flight there was no way I could get there in time. I pleaded with Allan, but he said the funeral director was adamant. No, they could not delay the cremation. I would miss my mother's funeral by two hours.

I was in a state the day I left. Jack drove me to the airport. We didn't say a lot, my mind was already elsewhere. What kind of a daughter was I? If I had stayed in Sydney, would Flo have still been alive? I was left with the feeling I'd failed not only my mother, my father and Jack but also myself.

I stayed with Allan for two weeks after Flo's funeral. The whole time I wondered if there was something wrong with me because I hadn't cried. It was as if I were bereft of all emotion. There seemed little point in returning to Moresby, but Jack sent a telegram saying he'd lined up a nice place for me to stay with two girls. One of them worked in the post office. Allan said it was best I go, so go I did.

For the first few weeks after my return to PNG, Jack couldn't have been more loving and gentle, just like he'd been when living in Sydney. Nothing was too much trouble—until the day he received the letter I'd posted to his old address in Mendi, three months previously.

I was back at the Post Office on the switchboard, doing the late shift and due off at 10.30pm. The post office management valued their telephonists and had kept my job for me. Jack phoned me at work, wanting to pick me up. He said we needed to talk about the letter he'd just received, and he sounded as if he were crying, or drinking. He was going on about how hurt he was by my words. He was hurt!

'Have a look at the date on the letter,' I shouted. 'It was written three months ago, when I hadn't heard from you for a month. We were supposed to get married in June, remember? It's now October, and you still haven't told me where you were. Think about the hurt you've caused me for a change, huh. And don't bother coming to pick me up after work, I'll catch the staff taxi.'

When I went outside after work, Jack was sitting in the gutter.

'Get up, Jack'.

As he lifted his face I saw tears running down his cheeks. I waited until he was standing, then walked towards my transport and turned back as I opened the door.

'I'm going home in the taxi, Jack.'

Jack arrived soon after me, stumbling out of the car and rambling on about that damn letter again. He felt like calling it off, he said.

'Good. Suits me. Just wait till I go inside and get the wedding ring. Here you can have this as well,' I said, pulling the engagement ring off my finger, and throwing it at him. 'I don't want them.'

He tried to say something, but I wasn't interested. Flo had been dead five weeks, and now this. Without looking back, I walked inside and closed the door to my flat.

Jack hovered in my life for the next four months, like a kite on a string. I could reel him in but I also wanted to let him go. The connection between us was strong, but my feelings were complicated by worry. The burden of my past was too big to step over or around. Deep down I had a feeling that only when I had found my birth family would I be able to marry and have children. And I was certain that someday I would do both these things and be happy. I should have realised long before that there was no room for a lasting relationship until I could face myself and deal with the mystery of who I was.

Finally, in January 1969, I made the decision to leave Moresby. My plan was to work on Green Island, near Cairns in Queensland. But then Jack decided he was throwing his job in and coming with me. We settled in Brisbane and Jack was like a starry-eyed teenager. He'd always been drawn to Brisbane.

'It's where it all started for us, Curly.'

He offered the rings back.

'Not like that, Jack. They have to mean something.'

Jack and I lived together for about a month. Everything seemed to be going so well, except I couldn't get a job as a telephonist, and became more and more anxious. I had run out of money and knew that if I stayed any longer I'd end up pregnant to him. And although having a baby was all I thought about, Jack wasn't ready to be a husband, let alone a father. According to him, we needed to sort out our 'communication' before embarking on marriage and parenthood. I didn't know how he proposed to do that, and I was still in the dark about those four unexplained weeks. Things weren't as good as he thought they were. Smiling that smile of his that had won me over in the beginning, he'd told our friends from Moresby who were visiting at the time, 'Can't live with her, and can't live without her.' We were addicted to—but destroying—each other at the same time.

Finally I came to my senses. This wasn't how I'd envisaged my life. I couldn't do it like this anymore. Not long after, one day in March 1969, Jack saw me off at the coach terminal in Brisbane. I was going to Sydney to spend time with my father. I had no idea if and when I'd be back. I hadn't thought that far ahead.

Lifeline

It had been eight months since my mother had died, two months since I'd left Jack in Brisbane, and meanwhile I'd made another trip to Moresby. Jack was working there for a few weeks and I'd gone up to see him. My intention was to sort our relationship out. We couldn't go on the way we were, living in different places.

I'd allowed myself three days, two for travelling and the other for Jack and I to thrash things out. Alas, Jack wasn't in Moresby, but somewhere in the Highlands, said the landlord. And no, he didn't know when Jack was returning.

I was back on the plane to Sydney before I knew it. My life had become a soap opera. I was twenty-six years old and chasing a man who just gave me the run around. Even Allan said he no longer respected me since this last trip to Moresby. He'd been pleased to see me back home in Sydney after I left Brisbane, but that was before I went off to PNG chasing Jack again. And because of that expense, I had no money left. I had to stay with Allan until I paid him back and saved some for myself.

The weather bureau got it right, the cold change had arrived. Despite the rubber seals Allan had fitted around the door frame, the wind whistled down the hallway. It was a chilly night and I shivered, pulling my knees towards me. Soon Allan would be home and he would light the kerosene heater. I had no energy to move, I was too busy examining the bottle of tablets in my hand.

Dr Adams had been quite firm.

'They'll help you sleep and settle you down. You can't go on like this, Lorraine.'

I had lost weight and I had dark circles under my eyes. My nails were bitten to the cuticles and bleeding, and I hadn't bothered to iron my clothes. I just wanted to sleep and be left alone.

Maybe it was all of these things that worried Dr Adams. He'd mentioned my thyroid gland and asked me to hold my arms out in front of me. Perhaps he thought I was a drinker and was checking to see if I shook or something. How could I tell him that I still hadn't grieved for my mother? Flo's admission to Rozelle, a place where someone with a brain tumour should never have been, and her death six weeks later was tearing me apart. What kind of a daughter and social worker could have allowed that to happen?

Sometimes it was as if I was on the outside of myself looking at a stranger, one who I had begun to hate and wish out of existence. There was a sensation I had when I was in the shower of wanting to melt and slip down the plughole. I couldn't go on like this anymore—it wasn't fair to Allan. Flo had taught me to always think of others before myself but that was the problem. Would it ever be my turn?

The answer seemed to be in my hand. Amytal 30 mgms. Take one tablet three times a day and one at night. What if I took four, just to see the effect, then I could swallow the lot and never bother anyone again. I wouldn't have to grovel for love or feel bad about myself, ever. I would no longer have to feel grateful.

My cousin Billy had done a similar thing the year before with his asthmatic medication. I went to his funeral. It was very sad. Back home, his three-year-old daughter ran through the house calling, 'Where's my Daddy?'

His father, Allan's brother, said he hoped his daughter-in-law, if she decided to get married again, did better the second time around. I winced when I heard him say that. My uncle was known in the family as a charming but violent man, especially to his wife and sons. Billy and I were the same age, we'd been good mates. I really wanted to ask him if he felt better now, if he'd made the right decision.

That year was all about funerals. First Billy, then Flo's sister, Aunty Joan. My favourite aunt, she died at the age of forty-six, from leukaemia. Two months later it was Flo's turn at age sixty. And now it was my turn. There was no age limit on dying.

Taking the plastic cap off the bottle, I counted out four tablets.

I heard footsteps coming down the hall. I waited for the key to turn in the lock. No, it wasn't Allan, but our neighbour. Pat lived in the flat opposite. She was easy enough to talk to, and had a son my age, but that didn't mean I wanted her to know my business.

The tablets were small enough to swallow without water. That was good because I didn't want to be distracted. If I wanted a glass of water I'd have to get up off the floor and walk into the kitchen and that was too big a job right now. My mouth was moist enough to swallow the four, moist like my face which was wet, although I had no idea I was crying.

I was reflecting on my life and what might have been. This time it would be Jack's turn to be left on his own, not knowing what was going on. Our relationship was over as far as I was concerned. He could wait as long as he liked in Brisbane or Port Moresby or anywhere, but I wouldn't ever be going back. Three times back and forth to Moresby in eight months was enough. I was sick of broken promises and being led on. If only there was someone I could talk to, someone who would understand and forgive the mistakes I had made.

I was drifting, drifting out on the ocean. What I needed was a lifeline, something to hold onto, to survive. I sat up quickly. Dear God, what was I thinking? I didn't want to end up like Billy. I needed help. I imagined my body down on the floor and my mind hovering somewhere above it. How could I ever have imagined dying alone on the lounge room floor? I needed help right now.

A sudden spurt of energy and I was reaching for the Yellow Pages on the phone table. I had to reach between both armchairs and, in my haste, the book fell out of my hands and onto the floor. I couldn't believe it. Of course. There was the very page I wanted. I called out in excitement. 'Lifeline.'

I grabbed the receiver and had to hang onto it for a while until I'd stopped shaking. I needed to compose myself. Then I could dial the number. Waves of tiredness washed over me but I was determined to hang onto that phone. My life depended on it.

The female voice that answered was soft and kind, and came so quickly I was caught off guard. My insides were crumbling into the mouthpiece. I didn't take in what was said or asked in those first few minutes, although I remembered afterwards.

No, I didn't need someone to come and see me, I was all right. No, they couldn't have my address, but my phone number was okay. I think they said something about phoning me back.

I put down the phone and it rang almost immediately. A man's voice this time. His was kind too, and he spoke with an accent I didn't recognise. I learned later that Louie was French, he was then the deputy director of Lifeline.

'What sort of people ring Lifeline?' I asked.

'All kinds of people.'

'So, I'm not mad then?'

'No, you are definitely not mad.'

By the time I got off the phone I knew that I didn't need to die.

Louie had made me promise that I would keep the appointment to see him the next day.

Counselling

It wasn't until our third appointment that Louie was able to draw from me the various pieces of my story.

'That's it,' he said pounding his desk.

He jumped up and began pacing the room. I studied his face but he moved so quickly it wasn't easy to see past his mood.

'An Afro-American father and the worry of throwbacks, eh? No wonder you are emotionally disturbed with all this going on.'

I leaned forward in my chair. Louie continued speaking and I suddenly had the impression that he must be angry. He sat down and proceeded to take his glasses off and wipe his face with his handkerchief. I could see he was concerned about me, concerned in a way I had never experienced before. I felt a flush of embarrassment then. It was like I was hugging to my chest the ragged facts that I had to live with, to endure.

The only time I felt right in the head was when I was talking to Louie, but even then I kept thinking of two words he'd said. Emotionally disturbed. It sounded serious.

I was on the outside once more, looking at myself. I made myself concentrate. I couldn't seem to stay within my own body. I could agree with Louie's analysis, nod my head in the right places, but in my heart, in my gut, I had this fear of being rejected. It was as deep as the ocean that fear, and as high as the tallest building. And there was something else, and this stemmed from my upbringing in white society. Did I want to know these people? Would I accept them? I simply couldn't act on his suggestion that I seek out my birth parents.

Even so, Louie had given me a lot to think about. Not only did he believe that I should look for my family, but he had suggested a joint counselling session with Jack. He was back living in Brisbane and the only contact we had around this time was when he would phone to let me know he was coming to Sydney. He didn't know I was seeing Louie and I doubted he'd consider counselling of any kind. His words of just a few months back still rang in my ears.

'Haven't you got over that yet?'

He was sick of hearing about my black father, and of me wanting a baby and marriage.

'Don't even think about it, Lorraine,' he said. 'As soon as we've worked things out, we can talk about getting married and having a baby.'

How much longer, I'd wanted to know. Twelve, maybe six months was his reply. We'd just have to wait and see. But we'd waited eighteen months already, I argued.

'I don't want just the one baby, Jack, I want more, because maybe then I'll have someone that looks like me.'

That had been one of our last conversations, in Brisbane, in March 1969, just before I returned to Sydney, and one week after Jack's thirtieth birthday. He did come to Sydney for a weekend in July, but he looked as downhearted as I felt. Nothing was resolved because we'd lost the knack of confiding in each other. He promised to return the following weekend, but changed his mind at the last minute.

People made promises they didn't keep. They told you they loved you and didn't mean it. That's why it was better and easier to bottle things up. By the time I met Louie, I was an old hand at keeping things to myself. It was best not to tell anyone anything, I decided, even Louie. Just tell him what he wanted to hear. Answer his questions.

I can see now that I was losing the centre of myself, the bit holding me together. All that was left was this hard shell filled with passivity, too afraid to speak up, letting others do it for me, smiling on the outside, crying on the inside. There was a voice inside me yelling. 'Speak up. Tell him, tell someone, how you really feel. Don't throw your life away.' But my lips were sealed.

Then Louie made another suggestion. About nursing. I hung

onto his every word. People looked up to nurses and nursing was a noble profession. I was desperate to get something right in my life, even if it meant living without love.

'You're right, Louie, I would make a good nurse.'

Next morning I phoned Crown Street Women's Hospital. I was hoping to enrol there and then and work with babies. Fearful of having my own rejected, I felt able and eager to love someone else's, no matter what their colour. Matron Love explained that it would be better to do my general training first. She advised me to train at Western Suburbs Hospital, in Croydon. The hospital was small she said, one hundred and twenty something beds, and friendly like a country town.

In October 1969 I enrolled as a student nurse, although it would be four months before I began my training. Matron Love was right. Western Suburbs Hospital was small and friendly. Everything looked bright, except for things with Jack. I decided I would let him go. We couldn't go on the way we were, with him in Brisbane for the past seven months and me in Sydney, both of us unwilling or unable to say what we really needed to say and hear from each other. I didn't know what the future held for me, but whatever it was, I had to face it on my own.

New Year's Eve came around. The end of the 'swinging sixties', the end of a long decade. What better time to phone Jack and let him know once and for all it was over. My friend Barbara was full of good suggestions where Jack and I were concerned. She was the older sister I never had. Pregnant for the second time, her life was together. It was obvious mine wasn't.

'Lorraine, if he was going to marry you, he would have by now,' she said.

Barbara and Louie were right—eighteen months was long enough for Jack to make up his mind. He'd persisted in saying my colour had nothing to do with it, and refused to elaborate, but he didn't have to. I reckoned that he still hadn't come to terms with my background. That was why I'd insisted he go to to Papua New Guinea on his own. I knew it was a risk. If he'd called things off because of another woman I could have handled it. But what I couldn't handle was his outright refusal to discuss the matter.

On the night he had proposed to me back in March 1968 Jack had bought two bottles of champagne and put them in Allan's fridge. They were still there. How ironic, I was about to toast the end of our relationship with the first bottle. I popped the cork and made the call just before midnight.

'Lorraine,' he said, 'I was coming to see you over Christmas, but you said not to.'

He was at it again. Him and what he was gonna do! His voice echoed down the line, as if he were under water. He didn't want to believe me. I repeated what I'd said. That I hoped that he would meet someone else and be very happy. I was letting him off the hook, isn't that what he wanted? Jack said nothing but I could hear him breathing. I waited a moment and then hung up.

It was a while before I realised what I'd done. I didn't want him meeting anyone else. I'd only wanted to shake him up, so that we might recapture what we had lost. But it was too late. He was probably already out somewhere getting plastered, like I was on his champagne. It seemed I'd be damned if I did, and damned if I didn't phone back. But I didn't want to be talked out of going nursing, and neither did I want to be apologising for the rest of my life as if everything that went wrong between us was my fault. No, this was the opportunity I'd been waiting for.

Nursing

It was a warm day in February 1970 when I first donned my uniform. The black pantyhose went on first, followed by a blue, button-through dress. Everything white was starched. I didn't mind the cap, the cuffs or the apron—it crossed over at the back and was fastened with large safety pins—but the collar rubbed my neck. Black lace-up shoes and a red cape completed the picture. We were the first intake for 1970 and the last group of trainees that would wear this old-style uniform.

It wasn't only the uniform that was old-style, but what went on behind the scenes as well. The constant bowing and scraping that was expected of junior nurses towards senior nurses and doctors took some getting used to. The jumping out of my seat when someone more senior entered the room, and everyone was more senior to me at that stage, even girls of eighteen and nineteen years of age. Fortunately, by the time I began my training the status quo was loosening its grip, but in those first early months I did wonder more often than not if I had made the right decision. After all, I was twenty-seven, an experienced woman of the world and not used to all these rules, regulations and rigidity.

This was the year Jack and I had planned on starting a family, and until it was over, I knew that emotionally things would be a struggle for me. A struggle between a body ripe for motherhood, and a mind focused on nursing.

Some in the nursing profession stood head and shoulders above the rest. Sister Rust was one of these people. 'Rusty', as she was affectionately called behind her back, was in charge of PW2, a private surgical ward. Rusty didn't ask staff, even juniors like me to do anything she wouldn't do herself. I admired her from that very first day I arrived on her ward, even before I saw her fetching a bedpan for a patient. Warm and efficient under that veil and steely grey hair, she more than anyone would have understood the struggle I was going through, if only I could have confided in her. But there was no need to, because my mind was already made up. Jack and I were over. I just had to get through this first year of training and it would be smooth sailing after that.

One day, when dressed in my street clothes after work and on my way out, a patient leaned out of MH1, a male public ward.

'My God. Why don't you look like that in your uniform?'

Grinning, I waved and walked on. I never did feel or look good in that damn uniform.

I had thought of nursing ten years earlier but didn't think I could cope with the discipline. It was four years' training then and nurses had to resign if they married—not the ideal occupation to encourage a social life. Shift-work, preparing and sitting for exams, living in the nurses' home, left hardly a free moment. A decade before the wages were too low to consider living out, and in the 1970s they still were. On my days off I sometimes stayed at Barbara's place, talking about the times when we both worked at the GPO. That past was a safe place to visit.

Most times, though I stayed with Allan in Redfern. Little by little I began noticing Aboriginal organisations springing up. One in particular sparked my interest—the Black Theatre. I wanted to go inside and check it out. I'd fancied myself as a singer, when I was younger. I was now more interested in acting or learning to dance. I lost count of the times I stood outside that building. Looking in, looking up, feeling excited yet fearful of being sprung by someone and asked to move on. I never hung around very long for that reason. I told myself I couldn't go in. That place was for Aboriginals, not for people like me with an Afro-American background.

How I longed for cultural connection with my roots, but I knew this could never be when my real father had no name. It would be like looking for a needle in a haystack—a big haystack in America. For the time being I had to be content with reading stories about American plantations and slavery, and learn all I could about Afro-Americans. I believed that in doing this I would connect to my father, if only symbolically.

I wasn't clear about my emotions at the time but I can see now that in choosing to be a nurse I was postponing, perhaps forever, the idea of becoming a mother. I was in a state of mourning—not just for Jack but also for not bearing and rearing a child. This loss haunted me and became more intense, even as Jack slipped further and further into my past.

The only way I could cope with this baby business, or should I say lack of, was to spend more and more time at Barbara's place, nursing and playing with her little ones as they came along. It was as if parts of me were screaming out for attention, and I found it impossible to think of anything other than wanting, longing to be in a relationship and becoming pregnant. I had to get a hold of myself. I was supposed to be training for a career. It was obvious motherhood would have to take a back seat, at least for the next three years.

I met Marco, a friend of a friend, in my second year. He was an Italian and a hairdresser. We went out together for four months. He wanted to marry me, but his mother had other ideas. He was the eldest and only boy in the family. She wanted him to marry another Italian, seemingly forgetting the fact he had already done that and come through a recent divorce. I left him to it. I later heard he married a German hairdresser. In fact, I nursed his wife a year or so after. I didn't know this until Marco and I collided on the ward one day. It was embarrassing at the time, but especially for Marco, who appeared to be in some shock.

In 1973 I passed my final exams and won the Mervyn Fletcher Award for outstanding attainment in practical nursing. I was so happy and pleased with myself, I couldn't stop smiling. Those years of training had been lonely, frustrating, challenging. At times I'd felt pushed to the limit, but it was satisfying to have achieved so much, despite my personal difficulties, and to have been rewarded as well. So, you would imagine that I was all set to do my midwifery training at Crown Street Women's Hospital.

Well, I did start at Crown Street, but three months later I was as fidgety as a fly in a bottle. I could not settle. Although I had so wanted to work with babies, I now felt trapped and suffocated. Royal Perth Hospital had a vacancy in their Post-Graduate Neurosurgical Nursing Course. I could learn about the type of brain tumour that my mother had had. It was five years since she had died. The opportunity seemed too good to turn down.

For the next six months we student nurses were surrounded by patients confronting death and dying—patients with head injuries, brain tumours and cerebral aneurysms, most connected to respirators, unable to breathe or do anything for themselves. We were young and so too were the majority of our patients. The job was demanding, the responsibility at times huge. Though all of us made it through, we openly admitted that this course had been the toughest we could ever face.

During those months of training, we were required to accompany doctors on ward rounds and do case studies on a particular disease related to our course. Ward rounds were for listening, observing, learning, asking and answering questions. We had to be on the ball. It didn't matter if our answers were wrong, just so long as we had a go.

I chose to do my case study on Jon, a thirty-one year old man with a pituitary tumour. As soon as he arrived on the ward, I knew what was wrong with him. I recognised the signs.

'How do you know he's got a pituitary tumour, Lorraine?' asked Kathy, one of my mates doing the course.

'My mother had one. The same squashy nose, spade-like hands, wide feet and severe headaches. Only she wasn't lucky enough to be diagnosed early.'

Jon remained positive throughout his hospital stay. The father of two young children and with a third on the way, he was prepared to go through anything to be rid of his headaches.

'Sister, I can't explain how bad they are.'

Thanks to Jon, I gained a better understanding of what Mum went through. But no matter how much I studied, my achievements dropped like stones in a bottomless well. I had another nursing certificate, this time in neurological and neurosurgical nursing but that didn't mean I wanted to specialise in it, or even continue my career in nursing for that matter. I was still dwelling on my past and that included my confused feelings for Jack.

For the next three years I kept moving, travelling—Tasmania, Melbourne, New Zealand and then back to Sydney. Still, no matter where I was living, I couldn't get away from the past. In that period I took any job I could get, office work, waitressing, whatever.

By 1976, I was at last ready to do midwifery. I didn't want to go back to Crown Street, so I chose St Margaret's Hospital, around the corner in Darlinghurst. I adored those newborn babies, their smell, the way their little faces crinkled around the eyes when I spoke to them. I marvelled at their differences, and the struggles some went through. A bit like me with final midwifery exams. I'd fail one, pass the other, sit again, pass the one I'd failed and fail the one I'd passed—until my third attempt. Then I passed both at the same time. Hallelujah! The nuns were ecstatic.

I had been warned about the nuns, and how hard they could be, but my experience of working with them was extremely good. They, and Judy Beavis, the lay deputy, encouraged, supported and never gave up on me. Twelve months later, I graduated and won a prize for the best case histories.

Itching to be on the move again, I took off for England, Scotland and then on to Europe. I had a career and three nursing certificates. But what for, and at what cost? I wasn't able to admit it, even to myself, but my life was sliding once again into the depths of despair. I was constantly afraid someone would be able to see right through me and call me the fraud that I was. I knew I should be solving the mystery of my ancestry, yet so much of my energy was expended in simply staying hidden from view.

Lucky

Many of my friends considered me lucky. Free of responsibility, of domesticity, free to travel the world, they said. Lucky? When there was no-one to keep me warm at night, no-one to share a beautiful sunset with, no children to kiss and cuddle. And the longer I put off the search for my birth family, the harder it was to muster the necessary courage to get started. Until I was able to take that step, my life was in limbo.

Living out of a suitcase for months on end on the other side of the world wasn't all it was cracked up to be. Nor was being a switchboard operator at a big London hotel. Yet, in order to change, to be more like my friends, I would have to hold myself up for scrutiny, be open to being judged. I saw rejection everywhere I looked. I expected to be labelled and cast aside.

When I returned home, I knew what needed to be done but I couldn't do it alone. First I needed to see Louie and have counselling, but I had just set foot inside Allan's door and was already wishing myself back in London. What had my father been up to?

'He's been shouting at the woman who lives in the flat opposite. She's frightened to go outside her door,' said Allan's best friend, Evelyn, who lived up the hall. 'Your father said she was trying to poison him with a gas cylinder. We don't know what's going on with him.'

That business about the gas cylinder sounded a bit far-fetched to me. Yet, before I left Sydney, I had noticed a distinct change in Allan's mood. The once happy and independent man had become withdrawn, dependent and miserable. Perhaps it was when I told him I was going overseas that he began to get anxious.

'What if I get sick while you're away?' he'd asked, in a whiny sort of voice.

'Dad, I hope you don't get sick, but if you do, contact Dr Mick and Evelyn. I'll be phoning every week, like I always do when I go away. I love you, remember? So, don't try this emotional blackmail on me, because it won't work. I need to get away for a while.'

Many years have passed since that conversation, but I remember it as if it were yesterday. And I remember, too, Allan sitting at the airport, shrunk in size and refusing to smile or engage in any way.

So, here I was eight months later, trying to work out what had transpired in the time I'd been away and what, if anything, I could or should be doing about it.

I decided to stay with Allan for a few weeks, to suss him out, before looking for my own place. Besides both of us could do with the company. All went well during those early weeks. Allan seemed happy and took delight in giving me breakfast in bed, which I hated, but didn't have the heart to tell him. He was almost like his old self again, so I returned to work at St Margaret's Hospital.

'You'll always be welcome back, Lorraine,' Sister Marietta had said, before I went overseas.

The following month I rented a bedsitter in Paddington, which was within walking distance of Redfern. Both suburbs were close to the city. The next time I saw Allan alarm bells began to ring. Who was this person called Tony who was giving him injections? And what injections? Allan said that Tony was a nurse.

Dr Mick knew nothing about injections either. And Allan's stories continued.

'It's those bloody people upstairs, they're trying to poison me with their nerve gases. They put their gas cylinder above the head of my bed. The bastards.'

'I can't smell anything.'

'I can smell it. I can, I tell ya.'

I tried to calm him down, but it was impossible. I'd seen him angry before but not like this. He looked as if he were about to implode. At the rate he was going I thought he might have a stroke. I decided to leave him for a while and visit a neighbour. It was the best thing I could have done, because when I returned, he was back to his cheerful self.

Over the next few days I noticed Allan's shuffling gait, the dull expression in his eyes, his slowed-down responses. I wondered if they were symptoms of Parkinson's Disease.

But that didn't explain injections, gas cylinders and a nurse named Tony. I was seriously worried. We had been through a lot together, my father and I, and I didn't want to lose him, not like this. He was only in his mid-sixties.

During my next visit I realised he was seriously ill; his condition had deteriorated rapidly. Alarmed, I phoned Dr Mick. He took one look and had Allan admitted to Rachel Forster Hospital. It was touch and go for many weeks. Allan survived, but he was never the same again, and not because he grew a beard that hid his smile. I was relieved that he didn't have Parkinson's, but the diagnosis was still worrying—schizophrenia.

Once the medical crisis was over, and Allan was on the right medication, he joined a day-care group for senior citizens. The group met once a week, played bingo, dominoes and other board games. They also made dolls from plastic bottle tops, held together inside with elastic bands. Bus excursions were arranged for picnics and barbecues. Although he had shed a third of his body weight and lost that beaming smile of his, my father was back from the dead and participating in life again.

His new friend was Russell, a much younger man, who was wheelchair bound. Soon, it was 'Russell this and Russell that'. When Christmas came Allan made two cards, one for his mate and one for me. Glued inside mine was a photo of the two of them, taken at a barbecue, accompanied by the words 'To Dear Toots, Merry Christmas, with love Dad'. I cried when I read it, realising how precious life is and how we should make the most of every moment and not leave it until it's too late to say 'I love you'.

With Allan on the mend, I turned my attention inwards. I phoned the silent number, the one I had memorised all those years ago.

'Louie works for himself now. Try this number,' said a familiar voice from the past.

I made an appointment for the following week. He was pleased to see me and we hugged like old friends. That day Louie mentioned an Aboriginal man he knew, named Paul, a couple of years older than myself. Paul had an identity problem as well, he told me. Would I be interested in meeting him? It seems he had recently returned from America where he'd been performing for some years with a well-known jazz group.

I nodded, but I would have been more interested if Paul had been Afro-American. But it was too late to back out. Louie had already phoned Paul while I was still in the room.

My home was still the ground floor bedsitter, for which I paid thirty dollars a week rent. Allan christened it 'Katingal', a reference to the maximum security prison at Long Bay in Sydney.

'Look at the bars on the windows and how dark it is, even during the day,' he exclaimed, reaching for the light switch.

Admittedly, it wasn't an ideal place for someone like me, who was prone to depression, but this was it. Darkness, bars on the windows and all. A recipe for depression if ever there was one.

Would anything come of this meeting with Paul, I wondered, as I checked myself in the mirror for the umpteenth time. If only I could say I was Aboriginal, maybe Paul and I could hook up together, although I couldn't understand why he had identity problems when he was Aboriginal and from Australia.

Trying not to appear too eager or desperate, I waited until he'd knocked a couple of times. A big smile greeted me when I opened the door. I was pleasantly surprised. Not only was Paul a nice person, and good to look at, but a top musician as well. When he sang, 'Feelings, nothing more than feelings', I felt as if I were the only one in the room, as if he were singing just to me. Maybe he was. We spent some great times together, but like so often before, the fear of being rejected was still uppermost in my mind and over the years we lost touch.

Mothers and Babies

Allan said Dr Mick was the best doctor he'd ever known, and recommended him to anyone who would listen—and pretty soon I was doing the same. I first met Dr Mick when he was looking after Allan, in the early 1970s. There was always a long wait to see him but once you met this man you somehow, instantly, felt better. His practice was in Redfern Street, not far from where my father lived, and over time he became a good and dear friend as well.

Sometimes Dr Mick and I would have a meal together and during one of these meals, in 1980, he asked if I had ever thought of finding my biological family. He knew I was nursing at St Margaret's, but I couldn't remember telling him before then that I was also working with relinquishing mothers.

Each time I accompanied one of the young mothers to the nursery, to see and hold their babies before signing the adoption papers, I felt I was walking in my biological mother's footsteps. It was easy to hug and cry with them. Nursing staff weren't supposed to be this emotional. But these girls were my least demanding patients, they'd ask for so little, yet each was in the process of losing so much. There were other mothers too. Those who'd given birth to sick or premature babies, or stillbirths, but those women did not pull on my heartstrings in the same way.

Working with so many mothers and babies helped fill the hole in my heart. Better than most, I understood what adoption meant. 'Please don't sign' I almost said on several occasions but stopped myself in time. Their baby's adoption was their business, not mine. At least they were given a month to decide, not like the old days, when single mothers were drugged to the eyeballs and shamed into giving away their babies. When the pain in my patients' eyes became too much, I would remind them of those four weeks.

Each and every day I was thinking more and more about my own origins. I looked at Dr Mick and nodded. I needed to find my mother before I wiped myself out with grog. Of course there was the usual list of questions in my head. Would the nuns at the hospital approve of my plan to search for my family? I hadn't even told them I was adopted. Would they have given me the job if they'd known, and would they now wonder if I was the right person to be doing that job day in, day out?

At last my decision was made, but I wasn't sure where to start. In the phone book the words 'Adoption Triangle' almost jumped off the page. I phoned their office, and spoke to Margaret, an adoptive mother, who proved to be a mine of information. She told me Adoption Triangle was a support group. It had started earlier that year. They had monthly meetings and there was one next week. Would I like to come? I quickly said yes, before I could chicken out.

The Triangle referred to the three sides of the adoption—the relinquishing mother, the adoptee and the adoptive parents. For the first time in my life it felt good to be adopted. Soon I would be surrounded by people like me, all searching for someone lost through adoption. I was about to embark on the most daunting and important journey of my life, not knowing who I would meet or where I might end up, but I was ready, like never before. If only the meeting were tomorrow, instead of next week.

I told Allan what I proposed to do. He nodded, and responded in his usual way.

'That's good, Toots.'

But his face seemed to tell a different story. Maybe he had second thoughts. He had nothing to fear, as far as I was concerned. Allan was my father, and always had been. I would keep reminding him of that.

Adoption Triangle

One night in October 1980 I walked into the hall in Werrington, near Penrith on the outskirts of Sydney. On the left, near the door, was a table. I counted three chairs. There were two people seated there, a man and woman, talking and flicking through papers. I assumed the woman was Margaret, the adoptive mother I'd spoken to on the phone. I recognised her voice. She exuded a bustling energy and looked like a person who would get things done. As I walked in she raised her head and smiled.

'Are you Lorraine?' I nodded. 'My name is Margaret and this is Graham.'

Graham stood up and reached forward to shake my hand and share his news. He had recently met his biological mother, and his wife had just found out she was pregnant. His grin was ear to ear. Congratulations were in order.

'Come, we'll get a cuppa. I'll introduce you to a few people before we get started,' said Margaret.

Jenny had recently met her mother, while Wendy was still

searching. Soon, Graham called the meeting to order. The hall was almost full, about forty people. Another woman, called Gloria, had joined Margaret and Graham—they represented the triangle of adoption. Gloria was a relinquishing mother, Graham an adoptee, and Margaret an adoptive mother. I didn't know their stories yet, but thought them courageous and strong to be dealing with the complex issues of adoption and for being our spokespeople. Already, I felt I belonged. It was better than family, I thought. Being among people who had experienced similar kinds of loss was comfortable. I scanned the faces around me. Some looked happy, others reflective or sad.

After the business part of the meeting was over, one by one members reported on where they were in their search, some asking for help. Adoption Triangle was not itself a tracing agency. We each had to find who we were looking for—but people helped each other, explaining what had worked for them. You didn't have to say anything if you didn't want to, and if you felt like crying it was okay. There was always a shoulder or two to cry on.

On the drive home I felt I was flying, my head was full of stories. I was fixed on the lies many of those present had been told. So what did that mean about my story? Maybe my father wasn't black. And maybe my mother had wanted to keep me, but had been forced to give me up.

Adoption Triangle had a contact register. My mother could register her name if she wanted to find me. I'd already registered mine. The Department of Youth and Community Services also had a contact register. Although they didn't search on your behalf, I put my name on that one too.

Jenny, Wendy and I had swapped phone numbers. If I was feeling down or had any questions before the next meeting, I had only to phone either of them.

The following day I visited Allan and told him about the meeting. He listened but seemed strangely quiet. At last he spoke.

'Toots, I want you to promise me one thing, that when you find your family, you won't drop me.'

It is many years since we had this conversation but I can still hear the emotion in my father's voice, and even now, it is hard to write about. Allan was pale, his eyes were brimming with tears. My mouth dropped open. I hadn't been expecting this.

'Drop you, Dad? I'd never drop you. You're my father, and I love you. And don't ever forget that. Okay?'

He looked at me, then nodded.

'I won't, Toots.'

So, you see, the search for my biological mother wasn't just about my feelings but my adoptive father's as well, and any others I had yet to meet in my biological family. I hesitated once again. If I continued, how many more times would I have to face this?

The ice might have been broken but I didn't want to discuss the process with anyone, except Allan, Dr Mick and my new friends at Adoption Triangle. Only with these people was I free to laugh and cry and be myself. I knew I couldn't mention what was going on in my life to my workmates. And if news of my search got back to the nuns, or the relinquishing mothers on my ward, how would it make them feel? Personally, professionally, it was a fine line to tread. Arriving home from work each day I'd be too exhausted to cook, and had no appetite when I did. Sweet sherry, savoury biscuits, cheese and half a pack of smokes was all I could manage. I lived in hope that my search would be short. At the rate I was going, my life might be too.

November's meeting, the last for the year, couldn't come soon enough and when it did one of the adoptees suggested I ask my doctor to write a medical certificate to Youth and Community Services, letting them know how my adoption experience was impacting on my health. A few heads around the room nodded. It was worth a try, so I went to see Dr Mick. He was pleased I was getting on with my search. He pulled out his writing pad.

Having something to focus on and think about relieved some of the pressure. Hopefully, February would bring good news from my various enquiries. Any news would do. But February came and went and so did March. And then a breakthrough, of sorts. Youth and Community Services appointed me a caseworker. His name was Terry. He sounded nice on the phone, and was a good listener, but no, he couldn't tell me anything about my mother. Surely, if he was a caseworker, his job was to help me find her. If not, what was the point in having him? It seemed like every step forward resulted in two steps back.

Crown Street Women's Hospital was my next port of call. I spoke to Bea, the social worker. She recorded my birth details and promised to phone back when she had something.

Another adoptee, Vera, had suggested I see a specialist at the Prince of Wales Hospital and have a blood test. She thought it might confirm or negate the Black American in me. This made sense. A good idea, but it was shameful as well. None of my friends had had to resort to a blood test like this, but I went ahead, determined to leave no stone unturned.

The poor doctor looked at me, mortified. There was no such test, she said. She talked with me for more than an hour and refused to take any money. I felt like a fool and cried all the way from the car park to my father's place.

'You can't give up now,' said Allan, rubbing his head, almost as if he were tearing his hair out. 'We'll find your family, we'll do it together, Toots.'

In the early days of my search, the relationship between Allan and I had become shaky. One day I even screamed at him to get out of my car. I was fed up with him, I said, acting as if he was my biological father when he wasn't. I just wanted some love and passion in my life. I wanted to find my real family.

It was hurtful to him, I knew. Allan often apologised for letting me down as a child, even though he had more than made up for it in recent years. He was still trying to make up for it, but often it was overwhelming.

Around this time, my caseworker, Terry, phoned with good news. I think he must have sensed my earlier frustration at his Department's inability to help.

'Lorraine, we've decided to help you find your mother. Lorraine...'

I don't remember my response.

Dr Mick assured me that finding my family was the right thing to do. He seemed to think I was coping well, but I felt desperate and asked him to refer me to a psychiatrist. The appointment was just one week later. The psychiatrist agreed with Dr Mick. He said my behaviour was normal under the circumstances, and that I wasn't going mad. He encouraged me to talk–until I couldn't stop–and laughed with embarrassment when I did. He gave me his card, told me to come back anytime I needed to. Even before I'd walked out the door of his office I knew I wouldn't need to go back.

Non-Identifying Information

Sometimes Adoption Triangle had guest speakers and this is how I met Joan Whetton. She was a social worker with many years' experience in the field. While her topic was 'Cross-cultural Adoptions', she announced that her talk this night would be the adoption of Aboriginal children.

I had been looking forward to this meeting. Cross-cultural adoption was something I could relate to, and possibly learn from. I had hoped Joan's talk might focus on adoptees like myself, with an Afro-American parent. I was disappointed to hear that it wouldn't but thought I would listen anyhow. Maybe Aboriginal experiences of adoption might be similar to my own.

Joan spoke about the taunts and racist name-calling that Aboriginal adoptees were subjected to, especially when their brown or dark skin didn't fit in with their white family's colouring. It sounded like she was talking about me. When she had finished, I rushed forward and blurted out my story. Joan asked my name and got me to write my details on a piece of paper.

'I'll be in touch soon, darling,' she said.

True to her word, Joan phoned the following week, from the far south coast of NSW where she lived with her husband. She offered me her support and encouragement and I can tell you we soon became good friends.

She suggested I write to Justice Michael Kirby. According to her I had nothing to lose and everything to gain. She had had some dealings in the past with Justice Michael Kirby, and thought highly of him. And while I was at it, why not write to the then Premier of NSW, Mr Neville Wran. People in powerful positions needed to know what it was like to be adopted and to be given the run-around. Maybe I could motivate one of them into considering changing the law. Their answers were prompt and polite, both wished me well in my search, but they had obviously failed to grasp my message.

Perhaps the *Sun* newspaper might be more understanding. I bought the paper most afternoons. So, why not write to them as well, I thought. The journalist who phoned in response to my letter was interested and sympathetic. He was an adoptive father himself, he said. He started the interview with a question. What could he do to be a better father?

'Just be honest, answer your children's questions, tell them you love them and don't send them away from home.'

He wished me luck, and that was the last I heard of him. Another dead-end.

I talked with Terry, my caseworker, but he was making slow progress and still didn't have anything to report.

About four weeks later I received a phone call at home. It was from Bea, the social worker at Crown Street Women's Hospital. Could I come and see her tomorrow, on my day off? Yes! And it was okay to bring my father.

I wore my cream silk suit and a vibrant contrasting shirt, hoping to make a good impression. Allan dressed up too. We told each other how lovely we looked, and made sure we had a supply of pens and paper to write down any information Bea might have. In the taxi to the hospital Allan opened a bottle of tablets.

'You better have this,' he said, slipping me half a Valium.

Soon we were sitting opposite Bea. A manila folder lay on the table between us. Bea had a determined look on her face. It was hard to know what she was thinking. She obviously wasn't adopted. I think I had already asked if she was.

My writing pad and biro were on the table. Bea looked at the pad, then looked at me. Everything was in slow motion. The information she was about to give me was non-identifying information, she said. I nodded, though I hadn't heard the term before. Hurry up, I wanted to yell. Just tell me my mother's name, so I can find her.

She opened the folder and began to read from the top of the page. My mother was born in Kerang, in Victoria. She was almost eighteen when she had me, and was living in an outer western suburb of Sydney at the time of my birth. My hand was shaking but I managed to write it all down.

'What suburb?' I asked.

'Sorry, I can't give you identifying information, Lorraine.'

'Then what about my mother's name? Can you tell me that?'

'No,' she replied and closed the folder.

Non-identifying information from documents, decisions and the like was intended to protect a person's privacy. In this case, my mother's. Well, that was all very well, but how did this social worker expect me to find my mother?

The Breakthrough

In a state of turmoil is the best way to describe how I mostly felt at this time—not the best state of mind to be in when making decisions, and nor did it allow me to reflect on the process of what was happening. I had been listening and acting on other people's suggestions and advice but not really listening to myself. The dead-ends were multiplying, until one day something bubbled to the surface. I'd begin with what I knew.

I had my mother's maiden name—Wooding. My first name was Gloria, the name my natural mother had given me. I knew where I was born, and how old my mother was when she had me.

Still needing help but more in control of my searching process, I became an amateur detective. I decided to write to all the Woodings in Victoria. Joan and my friends at Adoption Triangle thought this was a good idea, but not knowing my mother's first name was a problem. Someone suggested that Gloria might have been my mother's name and not mine. Authorities did that sort of thing to put you off track, they said.

Writing letters was easy for me, but this letter was different. I decided to make Gloria my mother, and tell people that I'd been a friend of Gloria Wooding's during the war, but we'd lost track of each other and I was trying to find her. I felt edgy, excited, and hopeful that no-one would ask me about what I did in the war.

The staff at the Mitchell Library were helpful and showed me where the interstate phone directories were kept. I copied sixteen Wooding addresses and phone numbers, by hand, out of the Victorian directory, and went home to write. All sixteen letters had self-addressed stamped envelopes inside. It was hard to concentrate at work, but at least I wasn't depressed anymore.

Eight replies trickled in. But it was the first, from Herb Wooding, that caught my eye. I had a good feeling about this letter. Herb didn't know anyone called Gloria, but his Uncle Joe Wooding in north-western NSW had a large family. He mentioned some girls' names and ages. The only one close to Gloria's age was a cousin of his named Hazel. As I read the letter I immediately believed I'd found her. I was sure of it. Hazel had to be my mother.

The only problem was my false story. Things could be risky. I now had to write to Herb and explain that I'd got mixed up with the name. It had been a long time since the war. Yes, it was Hazel that I was looking for, and not Gloria. Did he happen to know where Hazel was living now?

Herb's reply came a week or so later. He seemed to enjoy writing to me. He had only met Hazel once—twelve, or was it fifteen, years ago—but he included her address from that time and her married name. He went on to suggest I write to Hazel's father, his Uncle Joe Wooding. Herb gave me Joe's address. Uncle was getting on, he wrote, getting towards eighty. He also mentioned Bill Wooding, Hazel's brother, who came from Warner's Bay and was a builder.

I couldn't wait to share my news with Allan.

'If Hazel's my mother, which I'm sure she is, then this Joe must be my grandfather, and Bill must be my uncle. Isn't that great, Dad? I wonder if my grandmother is alive too?'

'Could be, Toots, could be. Let's hope so.'

~

One minute I was as high as a kite and the next I was in a black hole. Then there were all the in-between emotions. It was hard to keep a lid on it. Information that could have identified me had been withheld at every turn. It was time to phone Adoption Triangle again. Margaret was over the moon when I told her my mother's name and she suggested I look at the current electoral rolls.

I changed my clothes and hurried to the bus stop. It was a beautiful spring day, with the sun sparkling on the harbour. Soon, I would have my mother's address. I was so fidgety it was hard to sit still on the bus and even harder to remain seated in my chair in the Mitchell Library. Suddenly, there she was on the latest electoral roll—Hazel Lesley Cartledge. There was a street name and a suburb, near Gosford, on the Central Coast of NSW.

I stared at the name in front of me. The name I had been looking for. What was she like, this mother of mine with an unusual surname? Would she want to meet me as much as I wanted to meet her? What would she tell me about my Afro-American father? I hoped she didn't mind that I hadn't married and didn't have children. Most mothers I knew seemed to expect their daughters to provide grandchildren. I had, for the most part, come to terms with my childless situation but still had concerns about what other people might think.

I looked around at the dozen or so others in the library. I felt like shouting to the rooftop, 'I've found my mother, I've found her'. Quickly, I gathered up my things and walked outside. I didn't care what people thought of this thirty-eight-year-old woman, laughing to herself as she skipped along the footpath.

By the time I reached my father's place my feet were barely touching the ground. As soon as Allan opened the door he knew what I was going to say. I don't remember how long we stood laughing and hugging each other, I just knew how good it felt and how my life had changed.

The next step was up to Margaret. I phoned and gave her all the details.

'Leave it with us and we'll get back to you, Lorraine,' she said.

The waiting was unbearable. I needed to get away for a few days, to think of other things, to go somewhere I hadn't been before. I decided on Hill End, Sofala and Mudgee. Martha, a friend from work, offered to join me. I still hadn't told anyone at the hospital of my search, but on our fourth and final day, when Martha and I were having breakfast, and the birds were chirruping outside, my story came pouring out. I don't know what I expected. I looked at Martha, waiting for her answer. Her eyes were unable or unwilling to meet mine. Thank goodness, I told myself, that I'd kept this news to myself all this time. I couldn't wait to get in the car and drive home.

Years later, when I questioned Martha about her lack of response, she told me that there'd never been anyone adopted in her family, she had never known anyone who was and consequently couldn't think of anything to say. That later conversation marked the end of our friendship.

The phone was ringing when I arrived home. I picked up the receiver just in time. It was Margaret. My reunion had been set for three days hence, at the Patron of Adoption Triangle's house in Toukley, not that far from where Hazel lived. Fortunately, I was still on holidays. Frankly, I was too strung out to work anyway.

I rang Allan to let him know about the reunion.

'Good, Toots. We'll go together.'

It was countdown time. Allan suggested I eat at his place. I was too excited to think about cooking, and he wanted to make sure I ate something. I had just said goodbye to him and put the phone down when it rang almost immediately. It was a woman's voice.

'Is that Lorraine?'

'Yeah, who's speaking?'

'It's Hazel.'

'Hazel?'

'Yes, that's right. I couldn't wait until the reunion. As soon as Margaret told me your number, I had to phone and tell you what happened.'

Her words seemed to come in a hurry.

'I wanted to keep you and so did your grandmother. She was the one who named you Gloria. But Dad, your grandfather, said there were too many mouths to feed as it was and you would have to be adopted. It was his decision.'

That night back in 1981 when Hazel rang out of the blue, I listened intently to all she had to tell me.

I dragged the bar stool over and sat with my back against the wall, steadying my right elbow on the bookcase, the receiver close to my ear, not wanting to miss a word of what my mother was saying.

'What can you tell me about my father?' I asked her. 'I understand he was a Black American.'

'No, Lorraine, he wasn't. I didn't know any Black Americans.'

'Are you sure?'

I'd lived with this information for so long. Could I trust this woman to tell me the truth?

'Yes, I'm sure. Your father, Fred Harper, was white. He came from the Riverina. He was in the army, but he died years ago.'

I could hardly speak but waited for her to go on.

'You're the eldest of six, three girls, then three boys, and the eldest of fifty grandchildren. Your grandparents are alive, they live in Coonamble.'

'My adoptive mother said you came to our place in Marrickville when I was a toddler and that you wanted to take me back.'

'No. It wasn't me. I didn't know what your name was, or where you were living, although after the papers were signed, your grandfather did go down to Crown Street Hospital. He'd changed his mind but it was too late, you had already gone by then. We didn't talk about it after that.'

One minute I wasn't wanted, the next minute I was. I didn't know who or what to believe anymore. And who was the young woman that Flo had talked about?

'When I was young, people thought I was Maori,' said Hazel,

'but Mum's Aboriginal, and so were her parents and grandparents. I was one of the dark ones in our family, always in fights after school, and I finished up in Parramatta Girls' Home.'

I could barely believe what I was hearing.

'I was just trying to win Dad's love and approval, but I never did. He said I went about it the wrong way.'

Aboriginal! Did Hazel mean I was Aboriginal? I didn't want to be Aboriginal. How could I be something I'd never lived? Why couldn't I be Maori? I knew more about Maoris than Black Americans or Aboriginals. And why wasn't I told any of this information when I announced my engagement back in 1968?

Some time later I put the phone down. Allan had a lot of explaining to do. By the time I arrived at his place, I was so pent up my words jumbled around in my head.

'Who told you these lies, Dad? Tell me. Tell me,' I shouted into his face, until the whites of his eyes began to show.

He quickly stepped back.

'I wouldn't lie to you, Toots. I told you everything I knew when you said you were going to marry Jack. That's what your mother and I were told by the social worker before we brought you home from Scarba. They said we'd be sorry for taking you.'

'Shit, Dad, what kind of a person could say that? What was her name?'

'I'm sorry, I've no idea, Toots.'

'She's the one who should be apologising, not you.'

I stamped back and forth trying to damp down my fury. I wondered how many other people this person had lied to and if she'd ever stopped to think about what she was doing. There were tears in my father's eyes.

'Why, Dad? Why?' I shouted, shaking both fists in the air.

'I don't know, Toots, I really don't.'

The Reunion

It was still dark on that spring morning in 1981 when I rolled out of bed. Too excited to sleep, I'd been awake for ages—just five hours to go before I met my mother. My body was as weary as if I had been on night duty for a week but my mind was alert, although darting all over the place. What did you call a mother you had never met? How familiar could you pretend to be? Would she think me odd for not having children? I wanted her to be proud of me, not disappointed. I dressed carefully in a red paisley-print, two-piece skirt and blouse-like peasant top. I loved wearing red, it made me feel good and I sure wanted to feel good today.

Vera, the Patron of Adoption Triangle, had phoned and suggested I leave the car at home and catch the train from Central Station to Wyee, where she would be waiting for Allan and me. Always a stickler about time, my father was waiting in the driveway outside the block of flats where he lived, holding a bottle of champagne. He told me he'd rung for a taxi ten minutes ago. He was wearing his favourite sports jacket and brand new sports shirt—it was pale green. We hugged and complimented each other. Just then the taxi pulled into the kerb. Allan opened the back door for me.

'Central Station please, driver. Country trains.'

Once our seatbelts were fastened, Allan reached for my hand.

'Here, Toots. You better have this. It'll help you relax.'

It was half a Valium. I thought I already was relaxed, but I swallowed the tablet anyway.

By the time the train arrived at Wyee Station nothing seemed real. It was as if I were in a trance or had had too much to drink. What with meditating and taking Valium, it was a battle to get out of my seat. Having no idea what Vera looked like didn't bother me. There were only a few people waiting on the platform. Vera had to be the one with the grey hair pulled back in an old-fashioned way. Allan and I were the only ones arriving together.

'Here's the car,' said Vera, guiding us to it. 'I decided we'd take the long way home, around the lake. It's very relaxing, takes about half an hour.'

I didn't like to tell her that if I was any more relaxed I'd be asleep. And to this day I don't remember any lake, only Vera and Allan getting out and leaving me in the back seat. I was struggling to undo a seatbelt that wouldn't budge. I felt confused and abandoned.

By the time I was free and standing outside the garage, I didn't know what to do next. There was no sign of Vera or Allan. I decided to follow the path, not sure whether what was hidden behind the nearby bushes was the front or the back of the house. I looked in the direction of the fence. A dark-looking woman was coming through the gate, smiling at me. I remember thinking that if she was looking for someone, she'd have to ask next door because I didn't live here. Feeling vaguely irritated, I wanted her to go away. I didn't want to be distracted, I was about to meet my mother.

She kept smiling and getting closer. She was carrying a large bunch of brightly coloured flowers. They looked like stocks, larkspurs and something else.

I turned my head, thinking she might be smiling at someone behind me, but there was no-one there, except me. This woman kept smiling, as if she knew who I was, and now she was within arm's reach. No. No. This wasn't my mother, was it? Her dark skin reminded me of Maori women I'd met in New Zealand. For thirteen years I'd been thinking my mother was white, but then I remembered what Hazel had said on the phone. So many words and images flashed through my mind. My mouth tightened. That bloody social worker and her lies.

Hazel and I fell into each other's arms, and held on tight, too afraid to let go, to even speak. I don't remember what happened to the flowers, maybe they were hugged as well, because when we walked into Vera's kitchen, they looked as if they'd been through the wringer.

I was in a state of shock. There was a dialogue going on in my head, arguments back and forth, processing what I knew, what made sense and the reality of this woman in my embrace. My *real* mother wasn't meant to look like this—she was supposed to be white.

There were two seats left, next to each other. Hazel sat in one, and I the other. The man next to Allan was Hazel's second husband, John. My attention was caught by his rather large nose, which I tried not to stare at. Hazel introduced us. We shook hands and smiled. Vera busied herself, attending the flowers. Soon we were sipping tea and nibbling on sandwiches and cake. Vera had put a table of food in front of us. Perhaps it was nerves but we ate the lot.

I looked at Hazel. She was still smiling. I tapped her on the arm and listened as she talked about my brothers, sisters and grandparents. Her skin was silky and brown. I tapped, again and again, to make sure she was real.

'Don't worry. I'm still here, I'm not going anywhere.'

I watched the tears as they glistened in my mother's eyes. I didn't want this day, this moment, to ever end.

'Time for a toast,' said Allan and Vera, half-filling our glasses with champagne.

We clinked, holding our glasses high.

'Cheers,' we said, as loudly as we could, then fell about laughing.

Scarba Home, Sydney

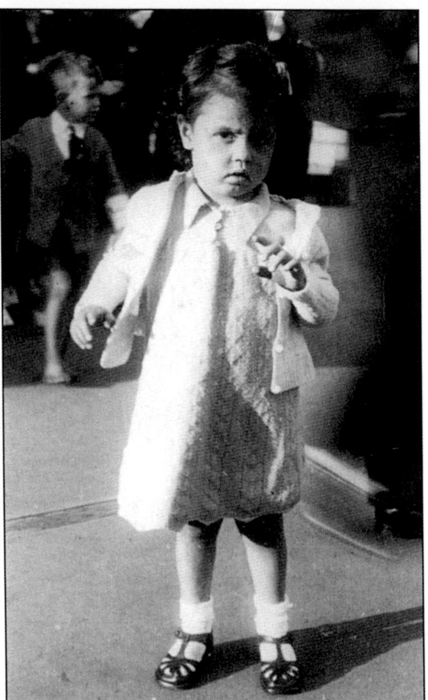

Lorraine, Sydney 1944

Lorraine, Dad Allan and cousin, Sydney 1947

Lorraine and Mum Flo, Sydney 1947

Lorraine learning to ride, Premer 1947

Lorraine and friends, Premer 1947

Lorraine in Allan's garden, Premer 1947

Lorraine, Rockley, Bathurst 1948

Isis River School (Upper Hunter), NSW 1951.
Top left, Lorraine middle row first on left. Top right, middle row, first on left.
Bottom left, sixth from left. Bottom right, third from left.

Lorraine, Isis River School Sprint Champion, 1952

Lorraine, Seven Hills, 1955

Lorraine, Waverley Station, Christmas 1958

Lorraine and her friend, Anne,
Waverley Station 1957

Bathing Belles, Kiama NSW 1962
From left: Lorraine and friends—Irene, Hetty and Sadie

Tommy and sister Lorraine, 1960

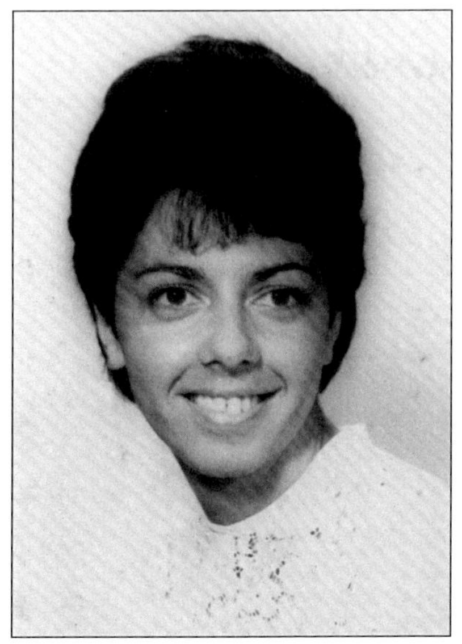

Lorraine, Sydney 1964

Lorraine (fifth from left) and friends ice-skating, Christchurch, New Zealand 1966

Hazel and Nan, Coonamble 1974

Lorraine's biological father, Fred Harper c1940s

Lorraine, aged 38, after meeting her family in 1981; and Hazel age 37

Allan and Lorraine, Midwifery Graduation 1976

Jeff and Tommy entertaining, late 1960s

Lorraine and cousin Shirl, Coonamble 1991

Lorraine and Tommy, Sydney 1996

Lorraine and Kevin, Roebuck Bay, Broome 1998

Lorraine, Lane Cove Women's Action and Information Group (WAIG), 1999

Lorraine and friend, Cameraygal Festival, Lane Cove 1999. The Cameraygal people are the traditional owners of Lane Cove.

Lane Cove Residents for Reconciliation Group, Harbour Bridge Walk 2000

Lorraine and Cate Turner, Harbour Bridge Walk 2000

Lorraine receiving the Inaugural Yabun Elder of the Year Award, Sydney 2008

Vera followed us outside into the sun. 'Before you go I want to take some photos of this special day. It's the best reunion I've had here.'

Soon Hazel and I were standing where Vera wanted us, posing as mother and daughter for the very first time. I looked happy in those photos, but underneath I was cracking up. Vera promised to send copies of the photos to Hazel, who in turn would send copies to me.

John and Allan were walking behind us. 'Don't they walk alike,' said John to Allan. 'She's her mother's daughter, all right. Look at their ears.'

There was a moment when Hazel made an odd comment.

'I hate red,' she said.

I didn't know what to say.

John suggested a celebratory drink at the hotel, near the station. We made our way there and sat at a table under the trees.

'We live down there,' he said, pointing through the bush. 'Can you hear the bellbirds?'

Allan and John went to fetch the drinks. Hazel and I sat quietly. There was such a hunger inside me. I really wanted to jump up and go to her, to hold her, to hug and kiss her but something held me back, something that told me this wouldn't be a good idea. In an odd way she seemed somehow fragile and small to me, as if I were her mother. She'd been through a lot, I realised then. I would have to be careful around her. I had waited thirty-eight years to meet this woman, and yet I was already baffled by the emotional distance that stretched between us. She seemed to be running hot and cold. But I'd cope. I was used to holding my feelings back,

I didn't even know what to call her—Hazel sounded disrespectful and Mum didn't sound right, because she'd never been a mother to me. We finally agreed that I call her Mother and she call me Daughter. But that didn't feel right either. I could feel her withdrawing, even as we sat looking at the photos and the family tree she had given me.

'This is Lorraine.'

'Lorraine? I have a sister called Lorraine?'

She smiled. 'Yes, Mum named you Gloria Patricia. Patricia, after your Aunty Pat. Lorraine started life as Shirley, but there were too many Shirleys in the family, so we called her by her second name, which was Lorraine.'

She turned back to the names on the family tree. The weight of history looked lopsided to me. All the ancestors were above my grandfather's name. His parents, grandparents, great-grandparents were all listed. Above my grandmother's name was a blank space.

'Now this is Jenny, Tommy, Jeff and Wayne, he's thirty and the baby in the family. He wanted to come today, but I thought it might be too much for you in one day. Would it be all right if we came to Sydney on Saturday?'

I nodded. But what was that I was detecting in her voice? Each time she mentioned my brothers, which was often, she was full of praise and love, but the same couldn't be said for my sisters and sisters-in-law. They hardly rated a mention and when they did, I sensed a lack of love or affection.

'Did anyone know about me?' I asked her at last.

'Only Wayne, and that wasn't until Margaret phoned from Adoption Triangle last week. Your grandfather said I wasn't to tell anyone. When I went to hospital to have you, he told the family I was having my appendix out.'

I didn't know whether to laugh or cry.

Family

Allan and I were on our way home. I turned the photos over and over in my hand, trying to match the faces with the names Hazel had written on the back. Lorraine, Jenny, Tommy, Jeff and Wayne. Faces so similar to my own, it was weird and intoxicating looking at someone so like myself for the first time. Each time I passed Allan a photo he nodded and said how alike we all were, but especially Lorraine and me. He thought my photos were lovely and that meant a lot. His approval was important, and I didn't want him feeling left out. He was gazing out the train window.

'You know you'll always be my dad. Nothing can change that.'

'Yes, Toots, I know,' he said, turning to face me with a smile.

I was consumed with love, happiness and sadness—all trying to find a space inside me. The sadness grew. I now felt motherless for the second—or was it the third?—time. I scolded myself for being sooky and precious. I reminded myself I was a grown woman but even then I knew I would never get over having lost my mother.

'And your father must be included in all the reunions,' Hazel had added when she said she was coming to Sydney with Wayne.

I was so pleased she felt that way. But I was still living a double life. I couldn't tell my work colleagues that I had met my mother Hazel. I was anxious about what their response might be. Raised eyebrows, maybe even laughter. At the very least there'd be lots of questions.

'Hi! What did you do on holidays, Lorraine?'

'Oh, I met my mother. And by the way, she's Aboriginal.'

Remembering my workmate Martha's reaction when I told her I was adopted, I kept my story close to my chest.

Hazel liked chocolate cake. It was her favourite, she'd said, so I bought the best I could find and had everything prepared for morning tea at Allan's place before meeting her and Wayne at Central Station.

Here he was, my youngest brother, eight years my junior and towering over me like a cuddly bear. Hazel introduced us, neither of us spoke, we just smiled and walked into each other's arms, hugging like there was no tomorrow. We might have still been there, locked together, had it not been for Hazel.

'I think we better get going. Your father might be wondering where we are.'

Wayne wanted to know how come his big sister was so short. I reminded him that I had turned eight the week before he was born and considered myself old enough even then to have changed his nappy. We joked about this and other things on the way to my father's, trying to make up for lost time, as if it were possible. I kept glancing at him in the rear vision mirror thinking how good-looking he was, and almost ran off the road. I wanted to immerse myself in all the stories I had missed. I wasn't keen, though, to know the politics of who wasn't talking to whom. Because I had created this perfect family, I didn't want to believe otherwise. My family would get along. They'd share and care about each other—not like my adoptive family or some of my friends' families. Look how well Wayne and I were getting along and we'd only just met.

Soon we were parked outside Allan's place and riding the fifteen floors up in the lift. Allan must have heard Wayne and me laughing and joking as the three of us came down the hall. We didn't even have to knock on his door, he was standing with it open, ready to greet us.

'You timed it nicely, the kettle's just boiled.'

He kissed Hazel on the cheek and shook Wayne's hand, his eyes moist with emotion. Later, I would marvel at the rapport between the two men—it was as if they were old buddies or father and son from a past life or something. With the tea poured and cake cut, we were soon tucking in—except for Hazel who seemed to have lost her appetite, even for chocolate cake.

When Allan asked Wayne if he'd like a photo of me, Wayne's eyes lit up. I guessed he might be too shy to ask himself.

Next minute, my father disappeared into his bedroom. When he came back he had a photograph in his hand. I was already blushing. The photo was of me sitting on a bloke's lap on a night out in London. I was carefree, happy, laughing at the camera. Before I could grab the photo out of Allan's hand, Wayne had already laid claim to it and no amount of pleading could get it back. Wayne shook his head.

'We could do a swap, I've got much better photos than that,' I assured him.

He waved it in the air.

'Not interested. I want this one.'

Already he was acting like a little brother, and like a big sister, I felt like throttling him.

At the Adoption Triangle meeting the following week, Allan and I were surrounded by my friends. They all said how happy they were for me.

'We can get close to you now, Lorraine. All those barriers have come down.'

Barriers? I hadn't even realised I'd put them there.

Soon we were all seated, and Allan and I were about to share our reunion experience, but someone was calling my name. An attractive, well-dressed, middle-aged woman was being ushered into the hall. She was smiling at me. Her name was Pat, and she introduced herself as my mother's sister. She was much lighter in colour than Hazel. She hugged and kissed me in front of everyone, and was laughing and crying. She hugged Allan too.

Later, Aunty Pat told me that she'd guessed the truth of Hazel's pregnancy. That rounded belly was no appendix! Aunty Pat decided to go along with the story. She told me Hazel had phoned her shortly after our reunion. She laughed as she quoted herself.

'So, Hazel, your appendix has turned up?'

Hearing this again, I was able to share in the joke.

But I wasn't laughing when I arrived home from work the next day, because the phone was ringing and it was Jack. He was in Sydney, and wanting to see me.

Since meeting Hazel I hadn't been able to get Jack out of my head. He was so connected to my past, I wanted him to know the truth of who I was. We had spoken briefly on the phone a few years back. Louie had said there was no harm in me phoning an old friend, so I did. Jack told me then that he had married in 1973 and that was the extent of our conversation. So, how uncanny that he should be calling me now.

'I have an Aboriginal mother, not an Afro-American father,' I told him.

He gasped and made some garbled comment.

We met that evening, and reminisced about what might

have been had circumstances been different. Jack had now been married for eight years and had a child.

When I mentioned my Aboriginality again, he didn't need to say anything. The shaking of his head and the sadness in his eyes said it all. Our conversation swung back and forth like our emotions.

'Why did you let me go so easily, that New Year's Eve in 1969?' I asked him.

'I thought you must have met someone else, that's why.'

It was then I told him about the last trip I'd made to Port Moresby in May 1969, when I'd intended to deliver my ultimatum. He had been somewhere in the highlands of Papua New Guinea at the time. Did his landlord tell him that I'd flown up from Sydney?'

'Yes, he did. And if I'd been there myself that day, I wouldn't have let you go—I would have married you there and then.'

There was no point in saying anymore. Jack would never know how close I'd come to ending my life that day not long after I returned from Port Moresby.

Up until now my thoughts about motherhood had been locked into the past along with this man, but faced with the reality before me, I knew it was time to let go, once and for all. I needed to get a life of my own, and Jack had to get on with his. Besides, there were all these family reunions ahead of me, and that was more than enough to cope with.

The Truth at Last

Within weeks the word had spread. Hazel's long-lost daughter had found her way home. My coming home was cause for joy, anticipation, celebration and explanation from my grandfather—who was now on the phone.

Joe was apologising as he struggled to make me aware of my mother's circumstances in 1943. I listened intently between his gulping breaths and his tears. There'd been too much water under the bridge for recrimination. I accepted his apology, thinking that there was no point interrupting him, to say how things had been for me. Unable to continue, Joe handed the receiver to his son Bill, next in line to Hazel. I don't remember anything Uncle Bill said that day but he sounded very nice on the phone. In the years to come I would enjoy his wicked sense of humour.

A few days later I received a long letter from my grandfather. Again, he apologised, he assumed that I'd had a good life. I felt as if I'd been struck a sharp blow. How could I explain to him, to Hazel, to anyone, that at the same time they were informing me about my family, they were also distancing me from them, and reminding me of all that I'd missed. I was the eldest child of this mother, this family, but I was the stranger in their midst, the odd one out. It hurt so much to live with that truth—caught between dreams that were high in expectation and a reality that was bruising in its intensity.

⁓

It wasn't until many years later that I'd find out more about the house in St Marys where the Wooding family was living at the time of my birth. Hazel had previously told me of the three-room fibro and corrugated tin shack with dirt floors, and that Joe had added rooms and verandahs when money became available. But Aunty Pat was able to tell me much more. She'd been almost twelve when they moved to St Mary's from Leeton. She remembers climbing onto the roof of the house to paint it, so that it wouldn't go rusty. The paint was a silver colour, she thought.

'You know, love, we had to water the floor before we swept it to keep the dust down.' She laughed at the memory.

'Imagine having to do that today! A bit later, Dad laid some Malfoid down.'

I asked her what Malfoid was, and how you spelt it.

'It's like a cheap lino, love, only dark grey or black. Everyone used to use it, especially if you were poor. It was made of tar.

'I was happier when it was just the three rooms,' she added, 'because we were all in together and not so spread out. We lived in that place for three or so years before Dad sold it. Then we moved to Swansea.'

I wondered if the house—the place where my mother went into labour with me—was very far from where Aunty Pat now lived in St Mary's.

'No. It would be about fifteen or twenty minutes' walk, I guess. Of course, it's not the same place that your grandfather built. There's a two-storey brick home on the block these days. The man who built it committed suicide, that was years ago.'

A shiver went down my spine.

'Geez, Aunty, I hope I had nothing to do with it. You know, my spirit being in the place and all, even if I wasn't there physically.'

'No, darling, I don't think you have to worry about that.'

Sometimes doubt consumed me. Had I really done the right thing in beginning this search, I asked myself over and again. Of course, I had made the right decision, just ask Allan, Dr Mick and my old mate Joan Whetton. And don't forget my friends at Adoption Triangle. Their words had a ring of truth about them.

'It takes time to get to know your family, be patient, you are doing fine, Lorraine.'

My adoptive mother would have told me that patience was a virtue, a quality I didn't yet possess. Maybe I was impatient, but there was nothing for me to gauge it on. I just wanted to be off this roller-coaster and tucked in cosily with my family. Then everything would be all right.

Allan had been so supportive throughout, but I wondered about Flo.

'Would she have approved of my search?' I asked him.

Allan didn't need prompting.

'No, Toots, she was afraid you might find your biological parents. You know what your mother was like. She didn't want people to know that you were adopted and that you weren't her own flesh and blood.'

I had had two mothers, and wasn't able to connect with either. I had failed as a daughter. But not according to my father, who was shaking his head.

'Toots, you didn't fail anyone, they failed you.'

When I told Joan I was meeting my grandparents, she asked if she could meet them too, as she had been a part of my search since I'd met her the previous year. Being a social worker, Joan had visited family of mine at Wallaga Lake community, outside Bermagui, near where she lived.

I had a lot of respect for Joan. Born in 1917, she was the middle child of eleven. Her mother was a journalist for a country newspaper. Whether it was the type of work her mother did, her

Catholic faith or Joan herself that influenced her to question and speak out for those less fortunate than herself, I do not know. But Joan was fearless, and spoke with passion, especially when confronted with issues of human rights, social justice and bigotry of any kind. Bristling, she would remark, 'I won't have that.'

Her association with Aboriginal people and adoption went back many years. She fully understood what I and many like me were grappling with.

More Relatives

The reunion with my grandparents and extended family was held at Little Bay. Allan, Joan and myself arranged to go with Hazel and John in their car. On the way, I could feel the tension building; so too was my excitement. Hazel mentioned names of cousins who'd be coming but, much as I tried to remember, very little stayed in my head. It would be a while yet before I met my other siblings.

It wasn't far from Redfern to Little Bay, near La Perouse, just a matter of minutes really. Everyone was talking and laughing, except for John who probably couldn't have got a word in if he'd tried. He pulled into the kerb, outside a small brick home that belonged to my cousin Shirley Ann and her family. I was reluctant to get out. Meeting one or two people was okay but could I cope with a big mob all in one go?

We were halfway down the concrete path when the screen door burst open and there appeared Aunty Pat, grinning from ear to ear. She spread her arms wide for a hug.

'Hello, darling, it's so good to see you again.'

Joan introduced herself.

'Pleased to meet you,' said Aunty Pat, still hugging me, while reassuring Joan that she was most welcome to join us.

Then she kissed Hazel and Allan.

'Hullo, cuz,' said a gentle voice coming down the steps.

It was our hostess, Shirley Ann, Aunty Pat's eldest daughter. Hazel had spoken of her with affection on the way over—I sensed they were close, closer than my own sisters. Shirley Ann had been a dancer with an Islander group a few years previously. I thought her beautiful, and still do. Everyone was laughing, polite, as we walked up the steps.

'No, you go first.'

'No, after you, Toots,' said Allan, nudging me in the back.

Into a sea of faces we went. And not one name tag.

I was centrestage, but I realised I didn't feel like running away. I smiled and nodded, acknowledging each introduction. I had to remind myself every so often that I was the eldest of fifty grandchildren, and my mother the eldest of twelve children. I was trying to take it all in. We later found out there was another grandchild, making it fifty-one.

My grandfather came towards me.

'Hello, love.'

I noted his shaky voice.

'It was me that signed them papers. It's my fault that you were adopted.'

He hadn't spoken distinctly but I thought I'd understood what he said. I wondered if he had his teeth in.

Hesitating, not sure what to say by way of reply, the words just tumbled out.

'Where's your choppers, Pop?'

This comment caused much mirth. My grandfather had his teeth wrapped in a handkerchief in his trouser pocket. He struggled to pull them out, then opened his mouth and slid the dentures in. He smiled, explaining he'd taken them out to eat.

'Do you always do that?' I asked, unable to keep a straight face.

'Yes,' he replied.

I held out my arms.

'Come here, Pop.'

His trembling body quietened and his anguish subsided. I held him until my grandmother came to my side and whispered in my ear.

'My darling Gloria.'

I pulled away from Joe and looked at her. I saw my brownness reflected back at me. Fancy being lied to about something as precious, and important, as this. The words were out of my mouth as though someone else had spoken.

'Aren't you beautiful?'

I touched her shoulder and then her face. She was wearing a powder-blue dress and a white cardigan, the colour blended well with her curly white hair. Those soft brown eyes brimmed with tears behind her glasses.

'You're beautiful too, Gloria darling.'

Yes, Gloria. I was Gloria. Overcome with emotion I had to sit down. Hazel was sitting by herself at a table, her head bowed. I couldn't tell if she was coping with all this. She seemed so alone.

But Joan had a great time that day. Every time I looked around the room, she was yarning to someone. Later, she would share her impressions with me, filling in the gaps of my skidding emotions.

Allan and Joe sat next to each other for much of the time. They were talking and laughing, but their eyes were on me.

There was a cake with pink icing. 'Hi Lorraine' had been written in white letters. I remember seeing my name marked out in silver around the edges. It sparkled like glitter. Beaming with pride, Shirley Ann's twelve-year-old son Shane stood beside his work of art. How could anyone cut through love like this?

Later, Shirley Ann gave me her photo albums to look through. Anything I wanted I just had to ask, she said. I couldn't get over how she and Hazel looked so like me when I was young. I belonged in this album. People were talking all around me but all I wanted to do was look at these pictures and imagine myself in this group, that group, or next to Nan and Pop, along with all the others. I can remember sitting there, thinking how my search had really begun when I had stared at photos of myself in my adoptive mother's photo album. Perhaps all along I'd known I didn't belong there.

Sisters

It didn't take long to work out that my mother's relationship with her daughters was a troubled one. Since before their teens, my sisters had fended for themselves. Sink or swim—they were on their own. They spoke of feeling left out, abandoned. Was this how our mother had felt behind the concrete walls of Parramatta Girls' Home? Did she also feel as if she had been abandoned? Already I had some understanding of her difficulties in nurturing her children.

Within a few weeks, my sister Lorraine was on the phone, apologising for the delay in making the call. When things settled down and the pressure was off me, she promised we would meet. She was looking forward to it. When I told her I didn't have children, she said that was okay, I could share hers, even though they were grown up.

'I'll send you some recent photos, what's your address?'

Our conversation flowed back and forth, interspersed with laughter. How easily our stories mingled down the line—it wasn't just a name that we'd ended up sharing, there were uncanny similarities in our life experiences as well.

Lorraine told me that the first six months of her life were spent in a home. When I asked where, she said it was attached to Prince Alfred Hospital. We wondered about this, and thought it strange that her name as 'previous issue'—that is as an older sibling—was missing on Jeff's birth certificate, which he had to obtain for National Service. Neither of us had the opportunity to check Jenny, Tommy or Wayne's birth certificates to see what was on theirs.

Seeing how alike Lorraine and I were, I did ask Hazel if Fred had fathered both of us. She neither confirmed or denied it. Her reaction was much the same as Flo's when I had asked her if I was adopted. Lorraine agreed with me that it was probable and later it came out that there were others in the family who were of the same view.

Lorraine had married her first love when barely out of school. Jimmy was many years older, and coincidentally had the same name as my first love. But not only that, her eldest son was called Allan, the same as my father. If I'd had a son he might have been christened Allan, as well. It was possible. The coincidences began to pile up—eerie, but comforting too.

It was a scorcher when I set out from home on the day Lorraine and I were to meet. I was running late. Not only was the humidity getting to me, but I was having trouble reading the street directory. I drove for ages in unfamiliar territory—wondering if I was ever going to find her. Lorraine's house was on the opposite side of the highway, but I couldn't work out how to get there, and each time I saw someone walking along the footpath that I might ask for directions, there'd be cars so close behind me I couldn't pull up.

After a number of detours and backtracking, I reached my destination. I was in a lather of sweat and needed to sit in the car for a while with the windows down to cool off. At last I gathered my things, wound up the windows, locked the doors and set off up the path.

The house was made of dark brick, with a small landscaped garden. I remember thinking it was the sort of house I might have bought.

'Hello,' said Lorraine and Jimmy, smiling as they walked towards me.

I was too excited to notice how alike Lorraine and I were dressed. It was only later when the photos were developed that I realised we were both wearing cream trousers and different coloured Hawaiian-print shirts.

'Sorry, I'm late. I got lost.'

'That's okay, you're here now and that's all that matters. Come inside.'

We talked all the way into the house, going from room to room, Lorraine giving a commentary and Jimmy backing her up, every so often. Everything felt comfortable and familiar, as if I had been here before.

'Let's go in the kitchen and have a cuppa.'

'I've got something for you, Lorraine. Here, hope you like it.'

'I don't believe it,' she said, opening the box. 'You couldn't have known this but I intended buying half a dozen of these very same coffee cups and saucers with next week's pay. I've already got the dinner set. Come, I'll show you.'

Sure enough, there in the large dresser in the dining room, was her Royal Doulton 'Old English Country Roses' dinner set. My jaw dropped open.

We were now in Lorraine and Jimmy's bedroom.

'I've got a pair of sandals the same as yours. But mine are beige. See,' she said, pointing to them on the floor.

'I generally buy beige, but I wanted a change this time, so I got these white ones.' I touched her arm. 'Maybe we were twins, but you were just slow getting out.'

We looked at each other, as if trying to imagine it, then roared with laughter. She was bent over holding her stomach, she was laughing so much.

'You mean I was thirteen months late!' she only just managed to chortle.

'Yeah. Something like that. It's possible isn't it?'

It was enough to start us off again. Laughing until the tears flowed. And that's how the rest of the afternoon passed. It was a day of discoveries. Lorraine and I learned we even had scars on the same parts of our bodies from childhood accidents. Like I said, it was eerie.

I stayed for a barbecue, cooked especially for me, by Jimmy.

'You'll stay the night, love, won't you?' asked my new brother-in-law.

He and Lorraine were smiling at me, making it difficult to refuse, though I was mindful of what Lorraine had said earlier. She didn't like people getting too close to her. She hadn't had much to do with our family since she married at sixteen, and so she wasn't used to being made a fuss of.

We'd got along so well Jimmy, Lorraine and me, but as I drove away, doubt nagged at me. I hoped I hadn't upset them by declining their offer of hospitality.

I was on a merry-go-round of family reunions, eight in all between September 1981 and February 1982, and I still didn't get to meet everyone. The first was with Hazel, followed by Wayne, my grandparents, cousin Shirl, Aunty Pat and several cousins, then Lorraine and soon after, Jeff.

Jeff had just got out of the shower at our cousins' place, and was still drying his hair when I arrived with Hazel and Allan. Jeff and I didn't need introducing, to walk into each others' arms. That's how it is with brothers and sisters.

And soon we were all at Uncle Bill's place with more aunties, uncles, cousins, nieces and nephews. It was hard to tell who was who, but what did it matter. We were family sharing food, love and laughter, and Jeff was singing and playing the guitar. It didn't get any better than that.

Identifiably Aboriginal

My mother, Hazel, was fourteen years old when she was sent to the notorious Parramatta Girls' Home. She was the eldest of my grandparents' children and at the time she was committed, on 29 November 1939, there were ten living children in the family. While Hazel was locked away, my grandmother gave birth to her eleventh child, Alice. Two weeks later Edward, the next youngest in line, died.

Some time between January and May 1940, Hazel and her father gave their consent for an operation. What sort of operation I still do not know. It was only after Hazel's death in 1994, that I was given the name of a contact at DOCS (Department of Community Services) who worked with separated families. If anyone could access records, this man was the one to do it.

It seemed to take forever, but it was only a matter of weeks before something arrived in the mail. A lot of the records had been destroyed since Hazel had been in Parramatta Girls' Home, I read in the letter. But this scant piece of information about my mother's medical history was finally in my hands. I wish that I could have asked Hazel—asked anyone—the questions that have been piling up in my head ever since.

It wasn't long after this operation, in July that same year, that Hazel absconded from the Home. Millie, an older cousin of hers who has since passed on, told me that Hazel was in Moama, on the NSW-Victorian border at the time trying to find Aboriginal relations of her mother's.

'Poor little thing, she was only a kid, wanting to find where her mob came from. I felt real sorry for her.'

I don't know how Hazel was traced but the police came for her not long after and took her back to the Home. The authorities then found her a job as a domestic, in Tumut in the Snowy Mountains area. She ran away again. Again they caught up with her—and again took her back to Parramatta. No date was shown for when she was taken back.

On 6 November 1941 my grandfather applied for her discharge and in March 1942 Hazel was finally taken home.

I have no doubt that her time in Parramatta continued to affect my mother all of her days. Hazel often referred to herself as the black sheep in the family. It made me cry inside because that's how I used to feel in my adoptive family. Her shame and pain were my shame and pain. She couldn't, or wouldn't, talk about what went on behind those walls at the Home. Her silence said it all.

Hazel was baffling, unpredictable and emotionally child-like. She had given up her first child but her idea of that child seemed not to have changed with the years. She wasn't really prepared for the adult daughter Lorraine.

Those who make decisions about children of mixed parentage, and especially Indigenous children, need to understand that when you take a child from their parent or their family, you rip a hole in the fabric of their personal history. The consequences can reverberate through the years and generations, and I often think of the difficulties many of my friends and workmates had when I told them I was Aboriginal. There were several friendships that I walked away from as a result. One was my old friend Barbara from my GPO days. She seemed to have trouble understanding my pressing need to find my family, and in accepting my Aboriginality.

'But you look so much like your adoptive mother,' she'd said, not even mentioning or acknowledging what I had just told her.

I wanted my mates to celebrate my Koori* identity with me, not to be silent about it, or to pretend that it didn't matter. And I didn't want them to ignore the fact that I was slowly coming to understand myself.

**Koori—term commonly used in most areas of NSW for Aboriginal person*

Tracing Ancestry

My biological maternal grandfather was christened Luddon Joseph Wooding but he preferred to be called Joe. Born in Victoria on 5 April 1901, on the banks of the Wimmera River about two miles from Dimboola Post Office, he was the youngest of six children. Joe was five years old when the family was forced to move into town so his father could find work. The new house had once been a butcher's shop. There was a big cellar beneath the shop and when the heavy rains came the cellar flooded. The Council insisted they move, stating that this decision was for health reasons.

The next house was about a mile out of town along the Melbourne to Adelaide railway line, not far from the Dimboola Cemetery. The family had the use of sixty acres of ground. Joe's father kept hives and his mother had a flock of twenty turkeys. These turkeys would wander back and forth across the railway lines and most days this was okay. One day, alarmed to see a train coming, they made a dash for it. Five turkeys got across, the rest were pulverised to a mass of feathers and bits of pimply flesh.

Joe's father died in 1910. One minute Joe was told his father had to go into Horsham Base Hospital for an operation and the next he saw him come home in a box the day before Christmas. They buried him on Christmas Day.

Each day Joe used to deliver cows for milking and was paid a couple of shillings for each delivery. It cost sixpence in those days to go to the pictures so Joe made a point of going once a month. Afterwards, the walk home was just long and dark enough to intimidate a boy who loved the excitement of the flickering screen. One night a local fellow asked Joe if he was frightened walking home alone. Joe replied that he didn't think there was anything out there to be frightened of.

Two weeks later Joe was making his way across the paddock when he saw a ghostly sight coming towards him. He dropped to the ground and remained still, hardly daring to breathe. The shape drew nearer but seemed uncertain where to go next. Joe began to suspect someone was playing a trick on him. He waited until the apparition had gone past. On the way home Joe couldn't stop grinning. He knew there was nothing out there to be afraid of. But it would be years before Joe found out who the prankster was.

In 1912, Joe's mother met a religious man, a widower with grown-up sons, and she remarried. The new, expanded family moved to Gerang Gerung, a town about twelve miles from Dimboola. Gerang Gerung was a thriving wheat centre. Big fields of wheat were common, up to twenty-six bags an acre. Joe liked his new school and his new home. He remembers those last years at school as being very good. He'd always played sport but football became his favourite game. He'd played the squeezebox since he was a small boy and later, when he bought an accordian, he used to take it everywhere with him.

Three years later, a few days after his fourteenth birthday, Joe left school. Two of his brothers, Les and Bill, had just enlisted in the army and joined the Light Horse Regiment. Joe got his first job later that year on a nearby farm, changing horses for the harvester and bag sewing. While the other six workers, all grown men, were earning eight bob a day, plus tucker, Joe's wages amounted to one pound a week. He used to say, in the years that followed, that this experience made him a Labor man. Joe could never understand how he was expected to do the same work, the same hours as the other men, yet be paid so little simply because of his age.

In 1916, three of Joe's step-brothers enlisted. All three were trained as machine gunners and sent to France. Meanwhile, Les and Bill were transferred from the Light Horse Regiment to Infantry. Les was sent as a sniper to France. Bill had it easier; he was training horses in the north of England. On 27 September that same year, Les was killed in action, in the battle of the Somme.

Joe worked away from home in the years that followed but returned in 1919 to be there when Bill came back. His three step-brothers arrived safe and well some time later. Joe stuck around for a while, working here and there, and when his chance came, put his name down in a ballot for some land. He was given a block eight miles out of Paruna along a sandy road. This was mallee country, desert country, surrounded by sand hills that looked like mountains. The first year's crop was okay but there was none the second year. So Joe moved on.

In 1923, he met Dinah, the woman who would later become his wife. She came from Barham in NSW, across the Murray River from Koondrook. In country areas during those times entertainment was mostly singing and dancing. One night Joe and a friend went to a singalong in Barham. The place was crowded. Joe's friend introduced him to Dinah and her sister, Lena. Joe and Dinah saw a lot of each other in the weeks that followed but there was no thought of marriage on Joe's mind. Then he got an out of town job as an axeman, felling trees and cutting them up to make way for the railway, not far from Moulamein. There were about eighty men in that crew and come Easter, most of them downed tools and went off in search of a good time. Joe had no money so decided to stick around. The boss asked if he'd like to earn a little extra money taking care of the lights. On some of the busier crossroads lights had to be kept burning all night. Joe was only too happy to say yes.

It was late afternoon on Good Friday and Joe had been checking lights. Coming back to camp he smelled smoke. When he got closer he could see the smoke was coming from his own tent. It was on fire. Everything inside was burnt—mattress, blankets, his clothing, the lot. He searched around in vain for his accordian. Joe had no idea how the fire could have got started. There were so few men left in the camp, he hated to think one of them had done this on purpose.

Turning away, he headed for the cookhouse and just as he got there a horse and sulky pulled up. There in the sulky was Dinah, Lena and her husband, Bill Harrison. They were on their way to Tulla Station and had come out of their way to see him. Joe had been writing to Dinah, had told her where he was working, but he'd not expected to see her again for some time, and certainly not out here. Distracted and pleased, he went around the camp borrowing mattresses and a big tarpaulin so he and Dinah could spend the night together. The next day Dinah continued on her way and Joe went back to work, but not for long.

When Joe broke the news to his workmates that he planned to get married they tried to talk him out of it. 'Don't be a bloody fool,' they warned, 'don't marry a black bitch.'

Joe had never liked to think of his wife as 'black' or 'Aboriginal'. As far as he was concerned her skin was as white as his. Of course, her parents and the rest of her family were dark, he knew that. But not Dinah; Dinah was different.

Joe continued working with the railway gang until the route had been cleared past Moulamein and into open country that led on to Balranald. It was August, time to leave, time to get married.

Hard Times

My grandparents were married in August 1924. They stayed around Barham for a few weeks but then moved to Kerang in Victoria. Joe bought a bike and got a job haymaking. Their first child, Hazel, my mother, was born the following January and the family moved back to Barham. A little while later, Joe ran into a station owner who asked him to do some fencing so the family moved again.

Joe now had a horse and, preparing for the move, he bought an old sulky. Setting up camp was easy enough. The weather was warm and they chose a good spot, near the dam. They'd bought hessian bags and set about sewing them one to the other to make a big enough covering. The frame was fashioned from stripped tree branches. The upright pieces had sharpened points at one end so they could be pushed into the ground and forked at the other to take the crossbar pieces. Extra support was provided by attaching knotted lengths of rope to the forked ends and stringing them across to nearby trees. A bed was made from thick piles of straw spread out on a carpet of leaves.

Dinah and Joe moved around a lot in the months that followed, chasing work wherever Joe could find it. He would remark, in his old age, how his dear wife never complained, not once. He would tell how her family had endured poverty and tragedy for many years and that Dinah must have learned early on how to make the best of things. Indeed, her father lost his sight the year Dinah turned sixteen. Although, he had a little vision in one eye it was not enough to enable him to get around unaided. Joe took his father-in-law, Ernest McGee, to Bendigo once, to see a specialist, hoping there might be something the doctors could do for him. Joe was told there was an operation that might help but it would be costly. None of them had enough to cover the doctor's bill, let alone the time in hospital.

The Woodings were still moving around at the end of 1925 but Joe had memories of a good Christmas, when they'd been living in an old two-room slab building down near a big water dam at a place called Green Hills, seven miles up the road from Hillston. Their first son, Joseph, was born in 1926 and they were full of plans.

Joe again put his name in a ballot, for a block of land in the village of Merriwagga and again he was lucky. He fenced the land then erected a dwelling. He had very little money for building materials so had to make do with pine poles for rafters and sheets of iron on top. The walls were made of bagged hessian. For the next four years Merriwagga was home. It was 1926 when they moved in and their second son, Henry, was born the following year.

In the village there was a school, bakehouse, a bank, clothing stores, a butcher's shop, a barber's shop, a billiard room, a blacksmith forge, a big public hall, ten houses on the main street and a hotel. Thunderstorms were common and no matter where Joe was, when he saw the first signs of a storm, he dropped whatever he was doing and rushed home. He'd aim to arrive in time to throw a wire rope over the roof and tie it down to steel posts driven into the ground. Even so, they did lose the roof on one occasion, along with a few temporary buildings Joe hadn't had time to secure.

In the dry spells, with westerly winds, dust storms and bitter frosts, sickness was rife. Joseph was eighteen months old when he came down with gastroenteritis. The nearest doctor was in Hillston, twenty-five miles away. It was a bitterly cold night and the doctor said he couldn't come out; they'd have to come into town and see him the next morning. This they did, wrapping the children in blankets before setting out in the sulky. Dinah cradled her son in her arms and did what she could to keep him out of the wind. They got to Hillston at 10am. Joseph died an hour later.

Dinah wept and Joe vowed to earn enough money to make their house more weatherproof. He could only find casual work and had to be a jack-of-all-trades. His next job was sinking wells and he helped to put down four in the district. The average depth for a well was between 120 and 160 feet. Layers of rock had to be blasted with gelignite but that wasn't the biggest problem. Once the hole had been dug below the quicksand level there was usually about three feet of what was known as 'slippery jack'. This layer was harder to penetrate than dense rock.

Well-sinking was dangerous work too. Joe once narrowly avoided an earth fall when he climbed out of a hole to make himself a cup of tea. Another time he'd cut the gelignite fuse too short and just as he was being pulled out of the shaft, he heard the explosion and looked up to see a windlass jump off its stand and land close to his head.

Another time Joe was asked to construct three 2,000-gallon tanks. The first one took him a long time but he was a fast learner. The next two went up in no time. Then Joe heard there was a job going in the village—grave-digging. It seemed at the time like a macabre joke but at least he could walk to work, he told Dinah. The cemetery had been created close to the village but as yet, there was no boundary line, nothing to mark it off in any dignified way.

In Joe's short time as a grave-digger, he dug six graves, three for children. Two of those children were twins. The third child was Joe's own son, Henry. First Joseph and then Henry. Dinah must have been a very anxious mother during this dreadful time.

Things got very bad after that. There was no money and no matter how far Joe travelled looking for work, he came home each night, his shoulders drooping with fatigue and Dinah knew he had no good news about a job. Dinah had a stillborn birth in 1927 but was soon pregnant again. Luddon William (Bill), another boy, was born in 1928 and Patricia came along in 1930.

In 1931, Joe struck lucky but there was one drawback. He had a job ring-barking, but he had to stay about eighty miles from home. Dinah went to Melbourne to visit her sister Lena and see a doctor about Bill's health as well as her own. She reported back to Joe that the doctor had admitted Bill to hospital and claimed that she, Dinah, had only two years to live.

Shocked by this news, Joe headed for the big smoke. He'd had to borrow money to make the journey and now he was running short. He met Dinah, went to see his son, then hurried down to the Labour Exchange near Flinders Street Railway Station. They issued him with a piece of paper that he had to present at a railway station for tickets to get home. Discharging his son from hospital, Joe prepared his family to return home the next morning. He was determined that this time fate would not intervene; he would make sure that Dinah and young Bill got better even if it meant leaving behind what they had, and looking for another place to live.

Dinah had sixteen babies, three of whom died in early childhood, and one who'd been a stillbirth. Added to this was the loss of her first grandchild. She had wanted to keep me and had already given me a name. But Joe had been adamant. Their three-room shack wasn't a fit place for a baby, and money was tight.

Joe and Dinah lived in many places over the years but finally settled in Coonamble in 1972. By this time their twelve surviving children were all married with families of their own.

In 1988, the year after Nan died, I was visiting Joe in Coonamble when we got onto the subject of my adoption.

Impatient with Joe, I asked, 'If you were too poor to keep me, how come you and Nan had two more babies?'

'Your grandmother didn't want to do anything about contraception. I tried asking her.'

'Well, what about you, Joe? Couldn't you have done something?'

He looked at me then, kind of shamefaced.

I didn't give a damn whether my grandparents' house had dirt floors or not. I just wanted Joe to stop thinking he'd done me a favour.

~

When Joe's autobiography was printed up in time for his ninetieth birthday in April 1991, some people reading it had to face the reality about their own identity, not as white Australians but as people of colour. Joe's daughter Pat and his grand-daughter Shirley had recorded him on tape a couple of years previously and Joe was excited about celebrating his big day with the launch of the book. One aunt was very puzzled.

'Lorraine, how long have you known you were Aboriginal?' she asked.

I was stunned. Hadn't she looked in the mirror lately? Her skin tone and facial features were obviously Koori.

'I've known since I met you lot.'

'Well, I didn't know until I read Dad's book.'

When I mentioned this to Joe, he replied that yes, his family should have known. It was obvious to me then that our Koori identity had never been made clear to our wider family. You had to be in the know to know. Like Hazel, who had worked out early that she was Aboriginal. She'd been called names and been involved in enough punch-ups on the way home from school on account of her brown skin which she got from her mother. But I still wondered why Joe wouldn't talk about it. And whether his silence had led to my mother's behavioural problems later on. I was indignant.

'Joe, our family should have been told they were Aboriginal. And that it was something to be proud of.'

He nodded.

'Yeah, love, I s'pose you're right, but it's a bit late now.'

It may well have been too late, but my grandfather is the person most responsible for my mother's incarceration. She too was a first-born daughter, her features more identifiably Aboriginal than her mother's. Her father seems not to have liked the constant reminder that he had married an Indigenous woman and it would appear that he expressed his displeasure at Hazel's expense.

Several members of the family complained to me over the years that it was impossible getting anything out of Nan regarding her early life. Many of them tried. I did as well. I took it for granted that my grandmother would automatically confide in me because I was her first grandchild and hadn't grown up in the family. Nan taught me not to assume anything. The only two relatives that she would discuss her past with were her nephews, Brian McGee and Jimmy Little. Whenever they called into Coonamble, Nan would grant them a private audience.

All along my grandmother seemed to me an outsider in Joe's telling of family history. I wondered if she really felt like that or if I imposed my sense of being an outsider onto her as I read Joe's life story. He distributed it to all his family at his party, but a month or two earlier, had handed me a copy when he was visiting family in Sydney.

'Here, love. I'd like you to have the first copy.'

Throughout this narrative, I have chosen to honour and respect my grandmother's spelling of her name. The signature that she used on her marriage certificate is Dinah Myrtle McGee. I refer to her as Dinah, and not Diana, as her name appears in Joe's story.

Nan may have accepted her lot when she married Joe Wooding. She seems to have made the best of things rather than fight for any kind of recognition. Tiny, hard-working, capable of keeping her brood in line when she had to, her life was hard and often lonely. She died in 1987, six years after we met. Two years out of those six, I was in Papua New Guinea. Nan and I didn't get to see a lot of each other in those remaining four years, because a six hundred kilometre barrier separated us. But on the occasions when we did meet, there were lots of hugs and kisses and I have treasured memories of us sleeping together and waking each morning holding hands. My grandmother had never stopped loving me, even when she didn't know where I was.

Although Joe was responsible for my adoption, whenever he was asked how many grandchildren he had, he added an extra one, so that my place was always kept. Different ones in the family have told me they used to correct him. It must have been confusing because none of them knew about me until I appeared on the scene when I was thirty-eight.

When Joe died on Boxing Day in 1991, four years after Dinah, it came as no surprise. In fact we'd wondered if he was going to make it to his ninetieth, which was a very big party, with friends and family coming from all over Australia. There were so many of us that day. We had colour-coordinated name tags—which I found very helpful. Joe had done a lot of the organising himself, with input from family and friends, but especially from Fay, his second youngest daughter who had lived with him since before my grandmother had died.

I visited Joe in Coonamble Hospital a few weeks before he passed away. He was attached to an oxygen cylinder, but seemed to derive more relief from using the nebuliser even though it was only temporary.

Joe knew he was dying. His house was in order. He'd even organised his own funeral. It was time to go—not that he ever said this but you could tell. Knowing it would be the last time I'd see my grandfather alive, and having forgiven him for signing me away, I read the poem I had written especially for him, called 'Grandfather Joe'. Soon after taping it to the top of his bed, I left.

A Second Proposal

Now that I had met my family and learnt the truth of who I was, it was time to address this lonely existence of mine. I had wasted twelve—or was it thirteen?—precious years running away from myself. In 1982 I was thirty-nine, and still hopeful of having a child, but not doing anything about it. If I wanted to be a mother I had better get a move on, because my biological clock was fast running out.

So where did women my age go to meet someone who wasn't married, gay or carrying baggage? I had been lucky in the past but that was when I was much younger and more men were available. Were there any nice ones left?

I decided to ask Marie, a nursing friend who had been married a few years and was in her thirties, for her advice. She suggested a blind date. Did she have someone in mind, I asked. Yes, his name was Kevin.

It wasn't love at first sight, but there was something about this man. We saw a lot of each other over the next few months, and Kevin made it clear from the beginning that my Aboriginality wasn't a problem for him.

'Stop worrying. I wouldn't drop you because you're Koori.'

Kevin had grown up in country NSW, and had mixed with many Kooris. He'd also lived and worked in Alice Springs, and been involved in some projects for remote Aboriginal communities. He was more aware of Aboriginal issues than I was.

Kevin worked for the Commonwealth Bank and had applied for a transfer to—you guessed it—Papua New Guinea. What was it about me and PNG? He said he'd forgotten about the application until receiving word that the job in Kavieng, New Ireland, was his. He'd already spent five and a half years on and off in other parts of the country, but not Kavieng.

'I've heard it's a beautiful place...' he said, looking rather sheepish.

We had been going out for seven months. I already knew that the drinking and casual lifestyle up there in PNG could be damaging to any relationship, particularly a new one. Kevin had applied for a two-year contract. The bank was expecting his reply by Monday, it was now Friday. He was due to leave Sydney in less than four weeks. If he went ahead of me and checked it out, would I wait, he wanted to know.

My answer was unequivocal. If he went on his own, he could stay on his own. I'd been through this separation business before, and had no intentions of going through it again.

Kevin frowned, smiled, then rubbed his forehead.

'Well, we better get married, hadn't we?'

I don't know who was more surprised by this turn of events, him or me. But it was full steam ahead after that. Not only were we happy about getting married, but excited about what lay ahead. Kevin's brother Brian was to be one of our witnesses and my sister Lorraine the other. She agreed on one condition: if I wanted her there I couldn't invite Hazel.

Things hadn't gone well with my mother, even from the beginning. Sometimes I wondered which one of us was the parent and which was the grown child. Hazel kept blaming my sisters for petty things that went back to their childhoods. What did any of this have to do with me, I wondered. My sisters gave me time to make up my own mind about our mother and didn't try to influence my thoughts or go on the way she did about them. I didn't want to side with anyone but it soon became obvious to me—as an outsider—that this family dysfunction wasn't all my mother's doing; it was multi-layered and intergenerational. Still, I found these outbursts of Hazel's very distressing.

I had never encountered anyone with such deep insecurities before, and while I kept dealing with the now, the present reality, Hazel was hearing and acting out something from her past, her childhood past, that kept her trapped in a cycle of subjectivity that none of us could penetrate. Like a lot of women in those days, my mother had had six children by the time she was twenty-six. By thirty-five, she was a grandmother. Maybe having children was Hazel's way of pleasing Joe—and society.

'I was always the black sheep in our family. I never could please Dad.'

In any case I understood Lorraine's strong feelings. She was scared of our mother and what she might do. Hazel had threatened to have Lorraine's marriage annulled, saying she was under-age when she wed. This happened one night at a public event where all kinds of accusations were hurled across the room at Lorraine, who by then was a sixteen-year-old wife and mother.

Kevin and I decided we would not invite Hazel to our wedding, regardless of my father receiving a letter from her out of the blue. I'd heard about these letters of Hazel's, and now we had one of our very own. It was June 1983, less than two years since my reunion with my mother, and just three weeks before I was due to marry and leave for Papua New Guinea.

'Look at this letter, Toots. She says you're not her daughter anymore but mine and she wants those reunion photos back. They were only on loan—not yours to keep.'

If Hazel's intention was to wound me with her poison pen she'd scored a bullseye. Her photos, without any accompanying letter, were sent back in the next mail.

With two days to go, this was no time for distractions, but time to buy a wedding ring. Kevin had invited twenty of his family, I was happy with my eight: Allan, Joan, Lorraine, Jimmy, my friend

Robyn, her husband John, and their two children, Kelly and Mark, my godson.

Lorraine saw me dressed in cream and breathed a sigh of relief. She was wearing dusky pink. It was then I told her that I had tried on an outfit in that same colour, but the style was too brief for a winter wedding, especially when my arm was inflamed from immunisation injections. I wanted something with sleeves and the only dress I could find was the one I was wearing. On our way to the church we were still chuckling about the possibility of us both showing up in the same outfit. We laughed again after signing the register when the priest who performed the ceremony asked how two sisters came to have the same first name. We never did get around to telling him.

Four days later, Kevin and I flew to Papua New Guinea to start our new life together. I'd only lasted six months the first time round, and Kavieng was very remote. I also wasn't sure if I'd be able to get a job. Papua New Guinea had had self-government since 1975 and Kevin said it was possible I wouldn't be able to work because the indigenous people of PNG had first choice of jobs. I had just finished working at St Margaret's Hospital and was burnt out, so a break would be nice, I thought, but not for too long. I wouldn't know what to do with myself all day having so much free time.

Circling Kavieng that afternoon in the Fokker aircraft, I was glued to the window, with Kevin peering over my shoulder, at the vista beneath us: the palm-fringed islands, the sparkling blue water and the white, white sand. How could anyone not be happy on this tropical island paradise? I had been given a second chance and was going to make the most of it. Not only was I loved, but I loved in return. There was so much to be thankful for.

The welcome we received was warm, like the climate, but the constant humidity sapped my energy. New Ireland was two degrees from the equator, I would need to slow down. That was hard to do. I'd been run off my feet at St Margaret's and here I was, still running.

Unable to get paid employment, I did some voluntary work teaching sewing to the kids at the nearby school, and got involved in other community activites too, helping out where I could. We were here to learn, to experience, to immerse ourselves. It was like one big extended family, all colours of the rainbow, thrown together, watching out for each other.

It was frustrating though, not being able to purchase everyday household items, a fact we took for granted back in Australia. But in the end these were minor distractions. We learned new ways of doing things and forged many good friendships. Kevin and I were told on more than one occasion how friendly and more accepting we were of the locals when compared to other expatriates.

'You're just like one of us,' they said.

Had I felt confident enough then and known more about my Koori background, I would have revealed all. But I had only met my family two years previously, and was anxious that someone might ask me questions about being Aboriginal that I couldn't answer.

That time in Kavieng went all too quickly and suddenly, two years later, the moment had come for Kevin to handover to John, the local man he had trained to take his place. John's family came from Bundi, in the highlands of Papua New Guinea. John presented Kevin and I with the most beautiful book about his people and where they came from. We treasure that gift and think of John every time we open it.

Turning Points

May wasn't the best time to arrive back in Sydney from the tropics, but Kevin's contract had finished and that was that. My list of complaints was long. It was too cold, people were unfriendly, and they drove too fast and too close to our car. I'd come from a place where people were kind and made time for each other, regardless of colour or race. Everyone mixed well. Okay, so you had to watch out for potholes, small children, falling coconuts or pigs wandering onto the road but...

I couldn't get over the conformity of 1985 Sydney and wondered why everything was done on such a formal basis, so different to Kavieng. Oddly enough, Kevin's response was just the opposite. He'd immediately felt at home.

One day I complimented a neighbour on her garden, thinking she would invite me in for a cuppa.

'You must come in for Christmas drinks,' she said.

But Christmas was seven months away. I didn't want to wait that long. I told Kevin that I missed our friends. He said he missed them too, but to give it time. Every second weekend Allan would come and stay. He was pleased we were home. Then Kevin was offered a transfer to Grafton, a promotion. He didn't think it fair on Allan so he declined and we stayed put.

There was a sense of urgency about Allan that I couldn't put my finger on. He hadn't been like this before we went to PNG, but now it was as if he were trying to cram as many experiences as he could into the shortest time frame possible. As if his days were running out. I felt like telling him to slow down, but at the same time I wanted to make up for what I hadn't been able to do for him while we were away. Perhaps, it was guilt, but I just wanted to spoil him for a while.

Little did I know his restlessness would soon result in the two of us flying to Norfolk Island for a week's holiday. When Allan first mentioned a trip, I suggested he ask his brother Rick to accompany him. But Rick, being Rick, made all kinds of excuses. If Allan had asked him five, ten years ago, he would have gone, but not now. He was too old. He had to look after his wife. In other words he didn't want to go. Hearing how disappointed my father was, Kevin suggested that I go in Rick's place. Both Allan and I were gobsmacked. Kevin even bought the tickets, and we were soon on our way.

Every now and then Allan would lapse into depression, so I'd remind him that we were on Norfolk Island, where he wanted to be, and that there was a lot to see and do, so we better get going.

Kevin had organised a small hire car, a manual, which was waiting at the airport. But by the time we arrived at our serviced apartment at Burnt Pine, I knew we'd need to change to an automatic. I couldn't seem to coordinate the gears, despite having driven a manual a year or so before. I could have persevered and worked it out but Allan was in no mood for me and my kangaroo hops. I got the giggles and couldn't stop, but at least it relieved the tension.

Before long we were motoring around the island, nice and smooth, slowing down for cattle that wandered freely across the road and had right of way. Allan seemed to enjoy these drives more than anything. He appeared awkward and distressed when eating out unless it was in a small place with few people around. Away from familiar territory he was out of his comfort zone. My father hadn't always been like this, of course. It was only since his psychotic episodes were diagnosed as schizophrenia some eight years previously.

It took a few days before I worked out that the best way to deal with Allan's withdrawal was not to pressure him. He didn't need to interact with others to have a good time, even if I thought otherwise. The idea was for me to focus on places that he enjoyed, such as the historic cemetery which was still in use. We spent many a quiet moment there, reading some of the heart-rending inscriptions and soaking up the beauty of the place perched above vertical cliffs. Both of us were drawn to, yet repulsed by, the old prison ruins and the history of brutality dished out to the inmates.

On the whole though, Allan seemed to enjoy his holiday and talked about it for weeks after arriving home.

Soon after our return, however, I had a very unnerving experience. One night at home, when I was cleaning up, I opened the cutlery drawer and it was as if I'd let a demon out. I remember taking a backward step and feeling a pain in my chest that was sharp, like I imagine a stab wound would be. I looked down, expecting to see blood. The next night the same thing happened. It was as if a magnetic force was pulling me towards the drawer and I couldn't control it.

I tried to give myself an explanation for what had happened and thought it might have been some sort of premonition. I had never before experienced such pain and I wondered whether it might have been a sign of heartache to follow.

I'd always been intuitive and I'd had premonitions before, although it was when I was much younger. On both occasions I had been on a bus and had witnessed two horrific accidents, two deaths. Now I had this same feeling again, but I wasn't on a bus, I was at home. I hadn't been scared while we were in Papua New Guinea but now I was nervous every time I left the house.

Meanwhile, my daily conversations on the phone with Allan had resumed. One day he told me he was in terrible pain.

'What sort of pain, Dad? Where is it?'

'In my groin.'

'Have you taken anything?'

'Yes, two lots of painkillers but they haven't worked.'

I didn't want to hear any more. My father never complained unless it was something serious. And I knew what that meant. It meant that I might lose him, and I wasn't ready for that. When I phoned Dr Mick he told me he had a long list of patients still to see but he would send a locum as soon as possible. Kevin and I drove to Allan's place as soon as we could. He was as white as a ghost and his forehead was damp.

Six weeks earlier, on Mothers' Day, Allan and I had visited Rookwood Crematorium and taped a white chrysanthemum on Flo's plaque. On the way home we had spoken about what we wanted done when we died. Allan wanted to be cremated and have his ashes near Flo's.

'What about flowers?' I'd asked.

'Whatever's in season, Toots. I'll leave that up to you.'

It wasn't until the doctor was examining him that I could see my father was easing towards death. Despite his pain, he looked peaceful—his eyes distant, as if he was already somewhere else. He was smiling and his skin glowed.

The doctor left and I asked Allan if he wanted me to stay or come back early in the morning. No, he replied, he wanted to get some shut-eye, he'd be here in the morning waiting for me. I kissed him on the forehead and stood for a moment looking at him from the doorway.

'I love you, Dad.'

'I love you too, Toots.'

He sat straight up in bed but his eyes were closed. I wanted to stay but another part of me wanted to run as far away as possible. Allan assured me he was okay and I waved at him and left.

Next morning I let myself in and hurried to his bedroom. His body was warm, but when I checked for vital signs there was no doubt. My father was dead. I kept kissing and talking to him, apologising for not being with him when he died. He was supposed to wait for me.

There was a small wooden box beside the telephone. He used to joke about that box and the contents. But it wasn't until the undertakers had been that I registered the box was there. Kevin drew my attention to it.

'What's in the box?'

All I could remember was Allan saying something about having enough for a rainy day. Even in death my father paid his way. He'd been saving for years. There was enough to cover all the funeral costs. We didn't need to add a cent.

The cremation was held on a Saturday morning. I remember standing on the front steps of the crematorium, waiting for Allan to arrive. It wasn't like him to be late. Next minute Kevin was by my side.

'We'd better go in now,' he said, gently steering me through the door.

It was only then that I realised why I was there. My dad was in that casket. He was the best father I could possibly have asked for. It was a good twelve months before I could say his name without weeping.

Bicentenary

The crowd is enormous. I am sitting in the lounge room. The TV is on. The cameras are panning back and forth from one vantage point to another. People are waving small Union Jacks. Some are smiling as the cameras zoom in on them. Others are caught unaware.

I feel the tension and excitement building, see it in people's faces, hear the emotion in the journalist's voice. It's the Bicentennial Celebrations—Australia Day, 26 January 1988. The world is watching as this country celebrates 200 years since the arrival of the First Fleet. Everyone is waiting. Waiting for the tall ships to enter Sydney Harbour, waiting for Princess Di and Prince Charles to arrive.

Our harbour is glittering on this magnificent sunny day. There is just enough breeze to keep the temperature down and assist the ships on their way in. Many brightly coloured craft and spinnakers, all shapes and sizes, are bobbing up and down. And here they come. They are beautiful but what do they signify? The First Fleet? For years it's been rammed down our throats—the

Bicentenary this, the Bicentenary that. I wanted nothing to do with it, but here I am in front of the box glued to the screen.

Now the cameras are panning the city streets. Splashes of red, yellow and black banners flash by as thousands of Aboriginal and non-Aboriginal people march together for peace, unity and justice.

I have time to read the words on one banner. 'Forty thousand years is a long, long time.' Yeah, right on. Look at those men and women wearing body paint. I call out to Kevin. He comes in and is standing beside me. He shakes his head. He doesn't know what it's about either. How come I didn't know about this? I'm Aboriginal, aren't I? And what does the red, yellow and black stand for, I wonder. Those colours do look good together, and especially on that flag.

Long after the television coverage is over, I sit thinking, thinking. Am I one of them? Where do I fit in? Do I have the right to define myself as Aboriginal? Does my upbringing set me apart in such a way that I can never find my way back?

There were tears in my eyes but before I went to bed that night, I made a promise to myself: I was going to to find a way of connecting with what I had lost, what had been denied me. I was scared, apprehensive, angry, but also excited.

The next morning I sat down with pen and paper. What did I already know? I had worked with three Koori women at the GPO back in the 1960s. I hadn't seen them as any different to anyone else. But there was a difference, surely. I wrote down their names, grateful that I could remember each woman so clearly. The private struggles of these women would not have been clear to me back then, but I now understood that there are so many challenges for Koori people.

I had on several occasions seen documentaries on television highlighting the appalling living conditions that Aboriginal people were subjected to in country areas. I remember I'd felt surprised, then shocked. I was puzzled. My adoptive mother may have fallen short in areas of mothering, but inequality wasn't one of her faults. She believed that everyone should be treated equally and that those who were more fortunate should share with those who weren't so lucky. This was the mantra I had grown up with, so the disparity between black and white, and rich and poor, came to me early, reminding me that all was not well in this supposedly egalitarian society that so prided itself on a fair go for all. 'Fair' being the operative word, it seemed. Mind you, I didn't do anything with that anger or unease; I just hung onto to it until the next documentary.

It's true, too, that I was so intent on figuring out why I felt different to those around me, I was in no position to speak out for others. Frankly, I didn't know how to be Koori, and the question hovered that it might turn out I wasn't. Like I wasn't Afro-American. I needed to be sure first. Too many years had been wasted believing I was someone else. But now with all these things I had learned, it was time for action, for speaking up and putting the pieces of my life where they belonged.

Taking up the pen again I jotted down my grandmother's name. Her voice had been silenced, maybe even before she had met Joe. Surely I owed it to her as well as myself to learn all that I could about her early life, our heritage, history and culture, and to share this information with our family. After all, I was her eldest grandchild.

I scanned the papers, both local and national, looking for anything to do with Aboriginal people or race issues that might assist my learning. A talk, a seminar, or book launch—anything to connect me to my grandmother and where she had come from. Maybe Joan Whetton from my Adoption Triangle days might be able to help me. I phoned, we chatted, arranged things, and soon I was on my way to see her in Bermagui.

Joan was one of those forthright women who had strong views about most things, and we didn't agree on everything by any means. But I had learned much from her, and this visit would be no different. We were sitting at the kitchen table having a cuppa, catching up, when Joan asked why didn't I contact Link-Up.

'Link-Up?' I said, trying not to sound resentful because, as usual, Joan knew more than I did. 'Never heard of 'em.'

She set about enlightening me. Link-Up was founded in 1980. It was based in Canberra, but later moved to Lawson in the Blue Mountains. To this day Link-Up works with Aboriginal and Torres Strait Islander adults who have been separated from their families as children and raised by non-Aboriginal people in institutions or private homes. Most grow up knowing little or nothing about their Indigenous heritage and culture. The work of Link-Up is threefold: to locate separated people who have not yet made their way home, or the families of people who have been separated; to assist people to come home, accompany them when they meet their families for the first time, and help them work through any problems that might have arisen; and to work with people who, despite having met their family, are still having problems coping with experiences they had as children after they were separated.

Before I left Bermagui that day Joan slipped me a piece of paper. On it was the name 'Coral Edwards' and Link-Up's phone number. Joan smiled as she said goodbye, telling me that Coral was not only the co-founder of Link-Up (with Peter Read) but a woman who would most certainly understand what I was going through.

Driving home that day I was lost in thought. On the one hand, I did want to learn so much about Aboriginal people; on the other, I felt my search for family was over despite what Joan said. She had met Hazel, my grandparents and Lorraine. I wasn't altogether sure that I did need Link-Up. I was convinced that it had little or nothing to do with me. I had already found my family.

Fancy That

It's hard to convey how fraught a process it is for an adopted person to reconnect with their background. I was like a character in a child's picture book—you know, those ones where you turn the page and a pop-up character springs forth, standing clear of the page. When the book is closed again, what happens to that character? Fitting in takes some doing; even today, right this minute, the gaps are more like chasms than missing links.

Coral and I spoke on the phone a couple of months later. I'm still not sure why it took me so long to phone her. The voice that said hullo was soft but also strong. I couldn't hang up. We talked and I was drawn in. We arranged to meet in Sydney the following week. (Years later Coral changed her name to 'Oomera' Edwards, although I always knew her as Coral).

'Where you from then?'

This was Coral's first question, almost as soon as we'd sat down. She already knew I came from Sydney and that my married name was Sippel. She smiled before asking her next question.

'Who are you related to?'

That was easy to answer. Jimmy Little is one of my mother's first cousins. Surely Coral had heard of him. She nodded then said something about putting me in touch with someone who would know my grandmother's family. I thought this startling, and clever as well. Her questions are familiar to me now though, as the way Kooris introduce themselves to each other. What's your name and where you from? There are Koori names that come from certain areas, a surname can suggest location.

Every six months Link-Up held weekend get-togethers to which everyone who had worked through Link-Up was invited. It was a time to meet new friends, look at the Link-Up albums, and share experiences and information with others. Coral introduced me to Belinda, who'd been adopted like myself. She was a fellow Link-Up member and lived nearby.

The amazing thing was that the more people I met through Link-Up the more family I picked up along the way. I was stunned by the number who'd been taken from their mothers and been adopted or fostered, or who'd grown up in institutions such as Bomaderry Children's Home, Cootamundra Girls' Home and Kinchela Boys' Home, in Kempsey. Two of my male cousins, Harold and Ian, had been through Bomaderry and Kinchela. One couldn't talk about it at all, while his brother just nodded and said, 'Damn shockin' place, Kinchela.'

Meanwhile I started tracking down autobiographies written by Aboriginal authors. I spent a lot of time in libraries and bookshops. I wanted to read stories about people like me, and to learn from their experiences. I had to know if I was on the right track, if I was thinking and acting like a Koori.

Coral encouraged Belinda and I to start learning our history, and to mix with other Kooris. We met Jack Beetson, who was both a lecturer and Executive Director at Tranby Aboriginal College in Glebe. Jack was fun and very knowledgeable. It was an exciting time. In the late 1980s Aboriginal culture was not mainstream, in any sense of that word, in the Australian media. There was a bookshop next door to Tranby, called Blackbooks. It was like a magnet to me. I couldn't stay away. On weekends I had withdrawal symptoms.

Belinda and I began an evening course on Aboriginal Culture. It ran for sixteen weeks and was meant for non-Indigenous students but with three babies under four, Belinda could only attend at night when her husband was home to mind the little ones. And I could only make it in the evening too. I was already working my butt off working weekends in a nursing home, as well as doing an Advanced Needlecraft Certificate Course three days a week.

At the end of the Tranby course there was a special camping weekend at Jervis Bay on the NSW South Coast. Jack couldn't stop laughing when he saw my tent. The friend I'd borrowed it from forgot to include the main pole. That was why it kept collapsing, Jack explained. I didn't know. This was the first time I'd tried putting a tent up.

'It's a real blackfella's tent, that one,' said Jack, clutching his sides.

'Does that mean I belong, Jack?'

'Yes darlin', you belong.'

That's all I needed to hear.

When the course finished I knew what my next step would be. It was time to contact my grandfather, Joe Wooding. I wondered what could he tell me about Nan and her family.

It didn't take him long to respond. His words accompanied me everywhere. If I wasn't reading his letter, I'd be talking to someone about it. From having no information about Dinah suddenly I had a great deal. I hadn't thought of visiting her country, but I knew now that I must. I phoned Coral to tell her my good news and ask if there was anyone I should or could contact. She gave me the name and phone number of someone in Horsham, Victoria, and also offered to take me down there herself. I thanked her but declined. This was something I wanted to share with Kevin. Fortunately, she understood only too well. I was taking my grandmother's spirit back home, she said. I hadn't really thought of it like that but yes, she was right. I was doing just that—and what an honour.

Before long Kevin and I were on our way to Deniliquin Caravan Park to camp the night. Deniliquin is seven hundred kilometres south-west of Sydney so we were very tired by the time we arrived. Joe had mentioned that prior to living in Barham, Dinah had lived on a mission near Deniliquin. I'd since learnt that it was Moonahcullah Mission. Early next morning, having no map, we set out in search of Moonahcullah and landed up on Cummeragunga Mission instead. 'Moonah', as it was affectionately called, had been closed down in the early 1960s. The Kooris had been kicked off and sent into Deniliquin, we were told. It was disappointing and embarrassing to find ourselves in the wrong place, though on our next trip Kevin and I were fortunate to meet one of the Elders who came back to live at Moonah, on the banks of the Edward River. His red motorbike was parked outside, and Uncle invited us in to share his fire and to tell us his stories of the old days.

But all was not lost on that first trip. Before leaving home, Lenoma (Clair) Jackson, a friend I knew through Tranby. gave me a message to deliver to Monica Morgan, one of the leaders at Cummeragunga. How pleased we were to find her at home.

Soon we were sitting around the table. Monica is a Yorta Yorta woman. My grandmother Dinah was too, she told me. We sat there for what seemed like hours, sipping mugs of tea and eating marble cake as my grandmother's history began to unfold.

Monica's narrative was informative and fascinating, filling in blank spaces. Dinah had not lived on 'Cummera' herself, she had left the district in the latter half of the 1920s. But her parents and some of her siblings had lived there well into the 1930s.

One of eleven children, my grandmother had lots of nieces and nephews scattered everywhere. They too had large families, some with six or more children. And so one connecting thread led to another. Some cousin or aunty would tell me I must go to Echuca and meet so and so.

'You must go to Mooroopna and Shepparton, there's a big mob of McGees living there. Make sure you meet Valda Jackson and her brother Lionel McGee. They were only young but were both a part of that walk-off from Cummeragunga Mission in 1939 because of starvation conditions and ill treatment by the white manager.'

Another cousin Barbara Day, from Echuca, could not understand why Joe or any of his children hadn't made contact with Dinah's siblings while they were still alive. The eldest girl Bella, Barbara's mother, was very upset. She couldn't understand why no-one had bothered, and neither could I.

'It was years before Mum forgave Aunty Dinah for not coming back to see her family. You're the first,' said Barbara.

What was really nice about this connecting business was being recognised and claimed as family.

'She's a McGee all right,' said one Elder in Mooroopna, glancing at me. 'Doesn't she look like Aunty Ettie?'

Great Aunty Ettie was one of Dinah's sisters. She'd had eighteen children. When I saw a photo of her, I thought, yes, they were right. I did look like her.

So now I could finally say six magic words: I am a Yorta Yorta woman. Fancy that! Soon after I changed my name by deed poll to include McGee in my surname.

'I'm so pleased you did that,' said my cousin, Betty Little. 'Now we know who you are when we see your writing. You are one of our family, and a strong Yorta Yorta woman.'

It was a confusing time, however. Cousin Lionel thought we were of the Pangerang mob while another cousin, Edna, had been told we were Wemba Wemba. I didn't know what or who to believe, so I stuck with Yorta Yorta and what Monica had told me in the beginning. But all three were close together on the Aboriginal map of Australia.

I hadn't yet heard of the word assimilation, let alone known that it was government policy, an attempt to breed Aboriginal people out. The only way I can explain this unwitting ignorance is that I'd been lost for so long not knowing who I was—and had been so self-absorbed with the not knowing—that it had somehow bypassed me that everyone in Australia was supposed to be white, which was what the White Australia Policy was about. I was a different person back then, a bit naïve perhaps. It's embarrassing when I think about it now because Kevin knew about these things in the sixties and he wasn't Aboriginal.

One of my Link-Up friends who'd been forcibly removed by the Aboriginal Protection Board, along with three of her siblings, said that what my grandfather did to me was worse than what the Protection Board did to her and her family. Grandfathers weren't meant to give you away; they were meant to keep and protect you. But hadn't Joe done that by doing what he thought best for me and my mother? It was a long time ago, when attitudes were different, and he was an old man now. I should simply forgive him and be grateful for any contact. He had apologised—and more than once. I didn't want to be eaten up with bitterness, I wanted to be a part of my family, and Joe was the head of it.

Her words were like a proverbial kick in the guts. Other people could tell me how it really was, but I couldn't tell myself. It was plain as the nose on my face. My grandfather hadn't wanted me. I could no longer deny it, but this understanding filled me with pain and anger.

Oddly enough though with each trip to Yorta Yorta country, these feelings began to dissipate. What the government and my grandfather had done was—is—unjust, but I told myself to put my emphasis on my Aboriginal roots. And in time, the pain and anger gave way to euphoria.

Family Tree

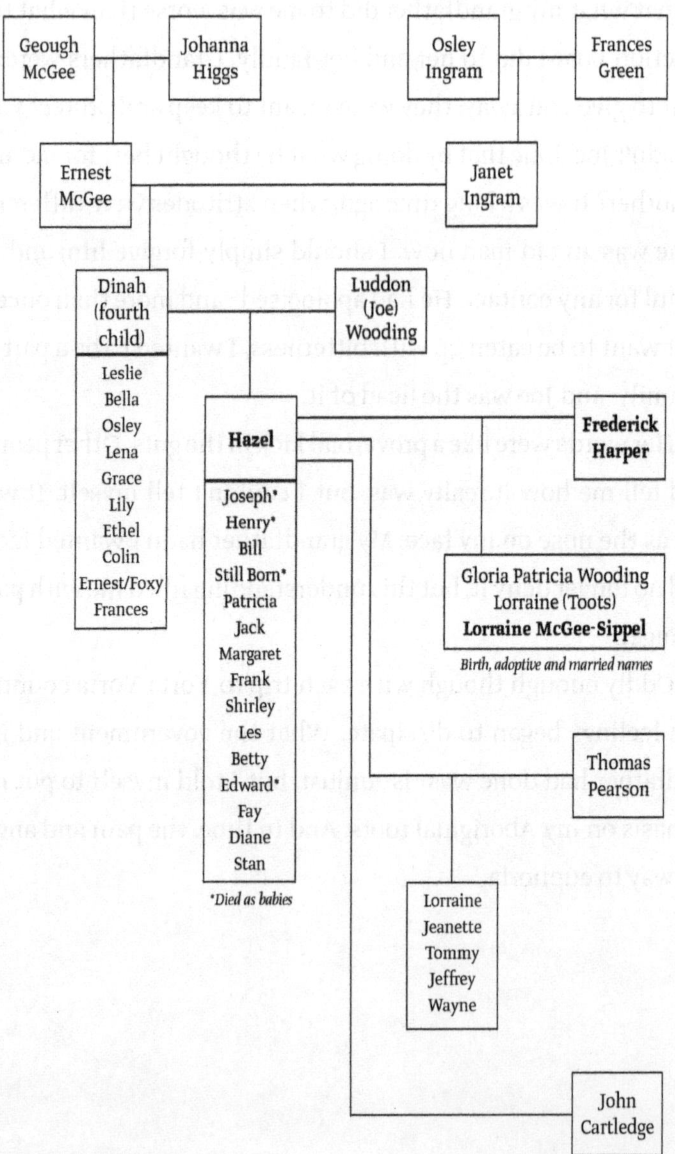

Geough McGee
Johanna Higgs
Osley Ingram
Frances Green
Ernest McGee
Janet Ingram
Dinah (fourth child)
Luddon (Joe) Wooding
Leslie
Bella
Osley
Lena
Grace
Lily
Ethel
Colin
Ernest/Foxy
Frances
Hazel
Frederick Harper
Joseph*
Henry*
Bill
Still Born*
Patricia
Jack
Margaret
Frank
Shirley
Les
Betty
Edward*
Fay
Diane
Stan
*Died as babies
Gloria Patricia Wooding
Lorraine (Toots)
Lorraine McGee-Sippel
Birth, adoptive and married names
Thomas Pearson
Lorraine
Jeanette
Tommy
Jeffrey
Wayne
John Cartledge

The Letter

During the years before my grandfather died, at the same time as I was following the trail that Coral was guiding me along, a letter—one of many—arrived from Joe. In this particular one he set out to answer some of my questions from a letter I'd sent him.

5 July 1988

Dear Lorraine & Kevin,

Mother's (your grandmother's) mother & father were a lovely pair. Her father was practically blind when I came into the picture as I took him down to Bendigo from Kerang in Victoria. When I first knew them they lived in a Kero Tin Humpy on the outskirts of Barham NSW. Most of their 10 children in all were born on a mission out of Deniliquin and most of his working life was spent on Tulla Tulla Station, North Wakool. After World War One, they shifted to Barham, that would be approx 1920. I knew her mother's father and mother, they also were a lovely old couple, their name was Ingram, her grandfather's name was Osley. Mother's name was Diana but apparently when I got her Birth Certificate the name was Jenny so it was never challenged. I was at her grandfather's funeral, it was a big funeral as he was very well liked in Barham. Her grandmother's name was _____ [name unknown] and she had only one uncle, his name was Henry Ingram. He was a returned soldier from the 1914-18 war and he was a great chap. He thought the world of your grandmother.

Now there is nothing else that I know of her mother's family & there is nothing that I can tell you about her father, only that he was a half-caste abo. He had a Scotch name, McGee, and her mother also of abo descent of both parents. They all were a wonderful family as far as I know but anymore I can't say. Mother's family from the eldest—Bella, Les, Dianna, Lena, Osley, Grace, Edward, Colin. One deceased. Now mother was the last living member of that family and deceased at the age of 81 years & 7weeks.

Now dear Lorraine—I can't tell you any more only that they were classed as half-castes but knowing her grandparents they were no darker than mother, and as I close this note I couldn't of thought as much of any other person as she was the best friend & wife & mother to all my children and I loved her for that. So now I hope this is all you wanted to know so wishing you & Kevin the best from your loving Grandfather

Joe Wooding xxxx

While I was overjoyed to receive this information about my family, I was also offended. The language my grandfather used! Half-castes, abos. How little he had learned or understood. Why not write Aboriginal in full, with a capital A? This was 1988, not the 1920s. I wondered if he still would have married Dinah if her family had been darker. And what would he have said if I told him how much it had upset me that I had been called a half-caste?

There were many things I wanted to say to this man, but thought better of it. I was aware of his age, and of me being the outsider. Kevin reckoned I was too soft on Joe, but I was panicky, afraid that having found them, I might lose my family again. I was determined not to say the wrong thing, simply to be grateful. Surely if I showed enough gratitude I'd be praised and loved. It mightn't have worked with my adoptive mother but that didn't mean I should give up on it.

The information Joe had provided meant I was able to visit the area where Dinah came from all those years ago. I wanted so much to walk where my grandmother had walked and to fill in the gaps that had kept me from knowing who I was and where I'd come from. The more I read Joe's letter, the more there was to question. His information was sometimes confusing and this was my grandmother that he was telling me about, so I was determined to get it right.

I already knew that Dinah was the fourth eldest of eleven children, not the third eldest of ten. And what about her sisters, Ethel, Lily and Frances? Frances was the youngest and later married Jimmy Little senior. She was only five years older than Hazel, yet Joe never mentioned her. And why did Nan's family leave the mission and what was the name of that mission?

Later, I would learn the answers to all of these questions, I would also apply for and receive Henry Ingram's (Dinah's uncle) war service record, from the First World War, but before doing that someone at Tranby recommended that I read *If Everyone Cared.* This was the autobiography of Aunty Margaret Tucker who had grown up on Moonahcullah Mission with her mother and sisters. I couldn't believe my luck. The more I read, the more I learnt about Dinah's family.

Aunty wrote with much affection about her old Uncle Osley Ingram (who was my great-great-grandfather):

> *Mother was working at Old Morago homestead, and we were in the care of a near relation, who saw that we did not want for anything and that we did not miss school. A week went by. We were still with the relation, who was old Uncle's daughter from his first marriage. The daughter had about seven children, some older than us and some about the same age. We were very fond of that family and looked upon the McGees as our nearest relatives on Moonahcullah. They had a beautiful flower garden and vegetables too in season.*

The McGees that Aunty mentions were of course Nan's parents and siblings. Aunty Margaret, her mother and sisters lived in the same house as Nan, her parents and grandparents. The relation who made sure that Aunty Margaret and her sisters went to school was Janet McGee, who was married to Ernest. Ernest, my great-grandfather used to call himself the black Irishman. Janet, his wife, was Nan's mother, and the daughter of Uncle Osley Ingram, from his first marriage.

Shortly after reading the book I met Aunty Gerry Briggs, Aunty Marg's youngest sister, in Shepparton. Aunty Gerry hadn't seen Dinah since she left Barham in the late 1920s with Joe and their baby, my mother Hazel.

'Stay right there,' she said, as soon as Kevin and I stepped out of cousin Lionel's car, that day in Shepparton. 'You look so like your grandmother, darling. We didn't know what became of her after she left in the horse and sulky with your grandfather that day. I'm so pleased you came.'

Soon the four of us were inside, sitting by Aunty's fire, listening to stories from the old days on Moonahcullah Mission and in Barham. Stories about my great-great-grandparents, great-grandparents, and my grandmother.

Between 1988 and 1995 I made five or six trips in all to my Yorta Yorta country—Nan's country. It was like Coral Edwards from Link-Up had said before I set out that first time. I was taking my grandmother's spirit home.

Five Funerals and a Wedding

On Sunday morning, 1 May 1994, Hazel rang her sister Pat to say she wasn't feeling well. By late afternoon my mother was dead. When Shirley Ann phoned I felt like someone who could have been on Mars. What did this death have to do with me? It was probably the shock, but I could not connect with my mother's death.

'What's wrong?' asked Kevin.

'Hazel's dead. That was Shirley Ann.'

I hadn't seen Hazel in the last few years, except at funerals. The most recent had been a few months previous, when Hazel's sister Shirley had died at the age of fifty-eight.

'Hazel's my mother, isn't she?'

I was trying to get my head around it. Then I heard this terrible noise filling up the room, somewhere between a scream and a groan. I wanted to make it stop, but I was reeling around the room. I'd lost her, I'd lost Hazel and now I'd never get the chance to say goodbye. It seemed I kept losing family when I'd only just met them and we were getting close.

My beloved sister Lorraine had been the first to go, in 1991 at forty-seven, then Joe, also that year, followed by thirteen-year-old Stephen, three weeks later, then Aunty Shirl in 1993. And now Hazel, at sixty-nine.

~

There was no manual that could teach those of us who'd been torn asunder from our roots how to deal with the pain. There was no guidebook to help or inform those who wanted, but didn't know how, to welcome us back.

Hazel's funeral was held a few days later, on the Central Coast. I had told Kevin I wasn't going, but he cautioned me.

'Are you sure? I think you may live to regret this decision if you don't.'

It wasn't until Shirley Ann rang the night before the funeral to say that they had a spare seat in their car and would I like to go with them, that I changed my mind. I told Kevin there was no need for him to come. I was going to my mother's funeral with my family. Kevin accepted this; he wanted me to go and felt that I was probably much better off going with my relatives than him. At least they knew Hazel's husband John, whereas he had never met him, and had only spoken about six words to Hazel.

Next morning, with tears streaming down my face I sat at the computer and wrote 'What might have been', a poem for Hazel. I was so determined to have it finished by the time Aunty Pat and Shirl arrived. There was no way I could go to my mother's funeral empty-handed. That seemed disrespectful to me. I also wanted my brothers to see my words and to read them. Only then might they understand how I felt and why.

The need to be alone with my mother, lying there in the casket, was overwhelming. There were people all around me, some of them trying to protect me from the starkness of this loss. I stood there wailing and pleading with her to know that I loved her and was sorry things hadn't worked out between us. I'd heard about women keening at funerals and had often wondered if that provided some relief. I think it must do because when I did stop, exhausted as I was, I felt I had let go of something, had expressed an enormous pent-up longing. I wondered where my brothers were, if they were coping, and how they might respond if they were to see the state I was in. It wasn't as if I'd grown up with our mother like they had. What if they needed comforting? I was their older sister. I had some responsibility towards them, didn't I?

Aunty Pat stroked my arm. 'Darling, they'll be all right. What about you?'

At some point I pulled myself together, but inside I still felt so terribly fragile. By the time my brothers arrived, I was more composed and we sat together in the chapel. Tommy and Wayne were either side of me, our shoulders rubbing together. I don't know why but I waited for my name to be mentioned in the eulogy.

The minister couldn't help but see me sitting in the front row. He rattled off John's name, Jenny who hadn't come. Lorraine who was dead. Then Tommy, whose daughter, my niece, got married not long after Lorraine's funeral. Jeff and Wayne. I think he even mentioned my brothers' wives, but not me. I didn't know whether to put my hand up, yell at him or what. If I had, I might have ended up in a blubbering heap. Whose decision was it to leave me out of the eulogy? Was it deliberate, an oversight, or just one of those inexplicable omissions that no-one notices except the person who has been left out?

Uncle Bill was sitting behind me, rubbing my shoulder. I reached back with my hand and squeezed his fingers. I had this feeling he was crying for me. I found out later that he wasn't the only one.

The wake was held at John and Hazel's place but hardly anyone came. My brothers' wives were busy in the kitchen cutting sandwiches when I arrived. A short fat woman was standing in the hallway. I'd never seen her before. Someone said she was a relation of John's. She was one of those people who can't understand why a member of their family would want to marry a Koori. Her voice was hard and ugly.

'When are these bastards going home?'

I felt like grabbing her by the hair and booting her out the door. It was hard to relax with that horrible woman lurking in the background. My brothers were near the clothes line in the backyard, smoking, deeply engrossed in conversation despite the cold and fading light. I wanted to be with them, for them to see what I had written.

'Hi darlin'. Are you okay? Come and join us,' said Tommy, giving a little shiver before stepping towards me as the others nodded. 'What you got there?' he asked, extending his hand.

'A poem for our mother. You can keep it if you like.'

'It's a bit hard to see out here,' said Jeff. 'Let me strike a match. My lighter's not working. There, is that better, love?'

We laughed at the absurdity of it all, Here we were, the four of us huddled together in a circle, out in the cold trying to read by the light of a matchstick, while we could have been sharing the light and warmth inside.

'That's beautiful, Lorraine', Tommy said, handing it back to me. 'You wrote that yourself?'

I could see he was impressed. I nodded, as I backed away.

'It's too cold out here. I'm going inside.'

I wanted to pat my mother's dogs but I couldn't find them. I also wanted to look in her room for the last time, but once I rejoined Aunty Pat and Shirl on the lounge I became aware of that woman again. I was no longer a mature-aged woman, but a lonely four-year-old, trying to make sense of what was going on around her. Too nervous to even move off the lounge.

'Don't worry. You've got more right to be here than she has,' said Shirley Ann.

John handed me Hazel's photo album. I could take what I wanted, he said, smiling at me. I thanked him and left with three pictures. I have since regretted not taking the whole album.

In my grief I'd forgotten to shop, and there was no food in the house when I arrived home from the funeral.

'What's to eat?' asked Kevin coming in the door, after work.

How I'd wanted and needed him to be there with me that day—but I'd also needed to push him away. I was scared at how I might react seeing my mother's body, and didn't know how he'd cope if I fell apart.

Fortunately Aunty Pat, who is a diabetic, had bought a bag full of doughnuts early that morning. She'd carted them around with her all day, in case we didn't get anything to eat at the funeral. So it was doughnuts all round that night for dinner.

Contact between me and Jack had been spasmodic over the years. He'd asked to see me again after we'd met up in 1981, but I'd just met Hazel and had a lot of processing to do. The next time we saw each other was in 1990. Link-Up were having a weekend get-together in the country. Jack lived up north so I'd contacted him.

At first the mood between us was strained, awkward, then over dinner something happened. The laughter, the easy banter. A bit like old times. He asked to see me again. At first I agreed, but I came to my senses when I arrived home in Sydney. I already had someone in my life, someone I loved and who loved me.

I didn't keep anything from Kevin, when it came to Jack. Both of us had been around a long time before we met. Just after we were married, Kevin received a letter from someone he had once gone out with. It worried Kevin more than it did me. I thought it was funny. What was wrong with an old friend making contact?

A few days after Hazel died, I felt compelled to let Jack know that I had just lost my mother and all these other relatives. He was a part of my journey, my story, having been with me on that awful night in the flat at Redfern in March 1968, when both of our lives were changed forever.

Hazel's ashes were supposed to be buried or scattered somewhere in Queensland with her husband John's, and not in the rose garden on the Central Coast where her funeral service was held. I didn't know this until years later, when my brother, Wayne, casually mentioned it over a meal. To this day I don't know where her remains are. But wherever my mother is, I hope she is at peace.

What might have been

No Mother
No more
No time for goodbyes.
Sadness within
For what might have been.

Too Late

Hazel had lived for a time with the husband who'd fathered four of her children. My sister Lorraine was slightly older than these four but was raised as his child too. Our brother Tommy, however, had not found favour with his father. His had been a brutal childhood, and the brutality had begun before he was old enough to walk.

Tom senior was a few years older than Hazel, a man respected or feared, depending on who was telling the story. According to Hazel, it was Tom who would get up and attend to the babies at night, not her. In the same breath she would say he was violent at home, yet charming to outsiders, especially women. My grandfather, on the other hand, described him as being the best of his son-in-laws; he worked, he cleaned the house and was a good cook.

'Yeah, but what about the violence?' I asked.

Joe didn't know about any of that.

Hazel and Tom enjoyed a drink and were keen on socialising. One thing led to another and soon there were ongoing fights within the home. Tom was good with his fists and taught his sons to drink and fight. He seemed not to have any understanding of how hard he punched or hit a child. And his favourite target was Tommy. Eventually he and my mother went their separate ways, but the damage was already done, especially to Tommy, a traumatised ten-year-old at the time of the marriage break-up.

I cried every time I heard the details of his story, and I heard it from various points of view. But my question was always the same: if people knew what was going on why didn't someone do something to help this boy?

Five months after my reunion with Hazel, I flew to Brisbane to meet Jenny and Tommy, my other siblings. I stayed with my sister and her family for two weeks and during that time I was made to feel very welcome. I was taken on tours of the city and hinterland, as well as on a trip to Toowoomba to meet Tommy and his family. This was in February 1982.

Tommy and I had spoken on the phone a number of times before meeting. When I told him I was his half-sister, he replied that there were no halves with him. I was his big sister, he loved me, and never to forget it. We learnt a lot about each other during these calls, including the coincidental connection Tommy had with my friend Barbara. Barbara, her husband and my brothers were living on the Central Coast and working in the building industry.

'Your brothers and I had many a barbecue at Barbara's place. I knew them well, darlin', nice people.'

Tommy would phone me on his way home at night from the public telephone box across the road from the pub. Four years my junior, he was the eldest of my three younger brothers, a workaholic and an alcoholic. Grandfather Joe Wooding said that Tommy could have been the best guitarist in Australia, if he'd had any tuition. I didn't get to hear him play until Lorraine died—he played at her wake, while our younger brother Jeff—the middle one of the three boys—sang. They harmonised so well together that night in the garage at Lorraine's place, and, as the saying goes, there wasn't a dry eye in the house.

I knew when we met that I wouldn't have him for long. That pain in his eyes was unmistakable. When our mother died, Tommy lapsed into depression. Hazel and he had shared a close relationship, as close as anyone could with Hazel. They both knew what it was like to be outsiders in their respective families. And being an outsider myself, I felt for both of them.

'Why did my father hate me?' Tommy would ask, over and over again.

I didn't know the answer, only that I loved my brother and didn't want to lose him. But lose him we did. He'd separated from his wife and was living alone, although they'd managed to keep the separation amicable and were good friends. He'd never raised a hand to any of his children, his own two, or the five his wife brought with her from a previous marriage. All the kids and grandkids loved him. What must have been going on in Tommy's mind that night when he hung himself? He rang our younger brother Jeff in northern NSW and told him what he planned to do.

'Wait for me,' pleaded Jeff. 'I'll be there, brother, wait.'

Being without a car, Jeff had to ask a mate to drive him. They drove as fast as they legally could, but it still was a trip of some hours. Jeff's mate had to force his way into the house. Jeff knew what they'd find and couldn't make himself go in. Tommy's body was still warm.

Like I said, everyone loved Tommy and we all knew Tommy loved his guitar. Jeff's mate, the one who drove him to Toowoomba and found our brother's body, went to the pawnshop the next day and paid the money to get Tommy's guitar out of hock. He knew how important this instrument was to Tommy and all the family. This was one hell of a good mate.

Scarba

In 2002, five years after losing Tommy, I began another search, this time for my biological father. When I had discovered that he was from an Anglo-Celtic background, the need to find him no longer seemed urgent or necessary, that is, until I started taking stock of my life.

I was getting older, obviously so was he. If I was meant to find him I had better hurry. He would have been in his early eighties then, according to Hazel. She was certain he was dead but I refused to believe it. Yet I hated to think he was in an old people's home, languishing due to neglect perhaps. Maybe he had even tried to find me and wanted to see his daughter before he died.

It was time to visit the Post-Adoption Resource Centre. Coincidentally, unnervingly, PARC—as it is often referred to—had its offices at Scarba in Bondi, that same place where, as a baby, I'd lived for six weeks before being handed over to Allan and Flo, my adoptive parents. Now a heritage-listed building, Scarba is no longer a children's home.

PARC was established by the Benevolent Society in 1991. Government funding was provided to set up a counselling and information resource for those affected by adoption in New South Wales and PARC has since gained a reputation for being at the forefront of post-adoption work in Australia and internationally.

My association with the PARC social worker had begun back in 1989, when we met at the launch of *The Lost Children*, a book about Aboriginal children taken from their families. We explained to each other how we came to be there. As soon as I mentioned my Aboriginality and being adopted, she asked if I'd be interested in being interviewed by one of her university students who was working on her final project. I agreed to do it. My contribution appeared in *Down the Track—Outcomes of Adoption Reunions*. The book was launched the following year, in 1990. And so over the years we'd kept in touch on issues regarding this topic.

Setting off that afternoon I was more worried about how I'd cope returning to the place where my story of adoption had begun, than finding information about my father or tracking him down.

The meeting was scheduled for 3.30pm. It was an autumn day, humid still as Sydney can be at that time of the year, but change was in the air. As we drove across the Harbour Bridge I remarked to Kevin about the clouds building up. I reckoned we were in for a storm.

We were twenty minutes early and waited in the car. Kevin reached for my hand. I smiled at him nervously, but I wanted to get in and out of that place as quickly as possible. I stood at the kerb while Kevin locked the car doors. He moved ahead of me to open the heavy metal gate, then we walked up the drive. The front door was locked. We pressed the buzzer and waited.

Painted in heritage colours of cream and green, the two-storey building appeared welcoming, even friendly. It was shadowed by a huge Moreton Bay fig that overhung the front verandah. I couldn't take my eyes off that tree. Would it have been here fifty-nine years ago?

The receptionist came and ushered us up a creaky staircase to an office. Inside was a high counter. She walked around to the other side, wrote in a book, noting our names, then directed us to wait in the hallway.

On the wall were two framed photographs, both of Scarba and taken back in the days when the upstairs verandah had been closed in. How long ago had the place been renovated, I wondered. There was no date anywhere. I had a camera with me and took a number of shots. One photo was of the building itself. The other had people milling about in the foreground. I was mesmerised. This photographer knew his craft well. I could feel myself being drawn into the frame, as if I were an invited guest, a witness to what appeared to be a garden party. The occasion spoke of a more genteel time when ladies wore long dresses, picture hats and carried parasols. Maybe it was just my imagination but I seem to recall dresses with bustles. It looked like it was a sunny day.

I wondered what time of the year it was and if the women were hot under all those clothes. The men, if I remember rightly, were wearing top hats and tails. So, Scarba wasn't just an orphanage but had this other history as well.

Later, when the social worker arrived, she led us into a small room and we got down to the business in hand. All I had to go on by way of documentation was my father's name—Fred Harper—and a possible address for him, taken from the electoral roll. Scant details, really. I also handed over a letter written to him, for her to pass on if and when she located him. I hoped this Fred was the one I was looking for.

The noise of the thunderclaps, and what now sounded like hail on the roof, was almost deafening. In the end we seemed to be shouting at each other in order to hear. It didn't seem right having to communicate this way, since we were dealing with such sensitive issues.

'Sorry,' I yelled over the din. 'What was that?'

There was no point. I looked at Kevin shaking his head. He couldn't hear either. We decided not to say anything more until the storm was over.

I looked at the high ceiling, the low rectangular coffee table, Kevin sitting opposite, the social worker between us. My mind was trying to imagine what this room, this place would have been like in 1943. I tried to imagine myself as a newborn baby. I didn't belong here. Where was my mother? I needed to be changed, fed and fussed over, but I couldn't be heard above the racket. There were all these other babies. Like little birds, with our mouths open, squawking in unison. But no-one was listening to us; none of us had a say in what was happening. Would any of us be able one day to refute all the lies our parents were told?

I glanced across the desk at the social worker. My earlier experiences with social workers had not been good. It wasn't just what had happened here at Scarba, but also that business when the social worker had recommended Flo be placed in a psychiatric hospital just because she had a brain tumour. Frankly, I'd found it hard to trust any of that profession until I met Joan Whetton in 1980.

'We weren't all the same, darling,' she'd said.

We had been in this room for well over an hour, discussing the search for Fred, giving as much detail as possible to the social worker. It was important to get this information right, especially as it was our first meeting regarding my biological father.

We were about to go when I turned to ask the social worker a favour. She was happy to oblige.

'I can't be sure, Lorraine, but I think the nursery might have been through here.'

My feet were heavy and my heart was racing, but I followed her. As I walked into the room, I became aware that I was not only here for my father, but for his baby daughter who had been taken from this place almost sixty years ago. Stepping forward, I felt myself reaching down into a bassinet and cradling my own infant self. My arms were across my chest. I was holding something precious that didn't belong here.

You are safe now, darling. You are loved and wanted. I am taking you home with me and Kevin.

Soon we were outside. The storm had abated. Kevin and I were simply amazed at the change. The air was clean and fresh, the rain all but a drizzle. We raced each other through the puddles like children, then stood in silence together at the gate, gazing back.

My Biological Father

Four weeks can seem like an eternity when you are waiting to hear if the person you have written to is the right one. One minute, I felt sure that this would be Fred, but the next I was full of doubt.

The same old question arose. Why had I left it so late? I might have met him years ago, but my adoptive father was alive then, and it wouldn't have been fair to him. Though we'd never discussed a search, I felt so much loyalty to Allan I could not contemplate such a thought. Fred was, by force of circumstances, a stranger. But he gave me life and had once loved my mother. Right then, that seemed good enough reason to look for him.

Kevin reassured me a lot during this period of waiting. It was natural to feel frustrated and sad, he said. I thought he looked frustrated and sad too. This man helped me so much to understand the nitty-gritty and to put things into perspective.

Inevitably, even more questions piled up in my mind, as they usually did. Fred mightn't know about me. If he had a family they might not know either. And if he were already dead, like Hazel had said, any surviving relatives might not believe that I was his daughter. How would I explain myself? For the umpteenth time I was reminded how hard it is being an outsider.

Many adoptees are happy with their situation, they don't want or have any desire to look for their biological families, and that's okay, because that's their adoption experience. There are others who, later on in life, for medical reasons, decide they need to know their genetic background. And there are those like me who feel driven to learn the truth from an early age. Fortunately, these days there is a more relaxed, open and honest approach to adoption. Thankfully, no more secrets and lies.

Writing to an elderly person sixty years on about something as sensitive as adoption can be fraught with danger. They could have a heart attack when you ask if they are your parent. Or like in one of those macabre jokes, they might even die on the spot.

I was earnest in wanting to respect the Harper family's feelings and I was treading lightly, as I had done when searching for Hazel. Luckily, the Fred I wrote to was more puzzled than anything when receiving his letter. I think he hung onto it for a while before showing his daughter. It was she who spoke to the social worker. It took four weeks to learn that this Fred wasn't my father.

The social worker and I concluded that my Fred might still have family living in the country town where I was conceived. It was her suggestion that I write to the local Family History Group in the Riverina.

'You never know,' she said, 'it's surprising what they know in country towns.'

I was so excited by this news I could hardly write. 'Dear Secretary...' I actually ran up the hill with the envelope, kissing the letter that Kevin had helped me to compose, and slipped it into the postbox.

The next day I sent two emails, one to the *National Indigenous Times* and one to the *Koori Mail*. Both are Indigenous newspapers, with enquiry sections where an individual or a group can provide details and ask if anyone has any more information about their family roots. With each letter and inquiry I felt more attached to Fred. Nothing ever came from these queries but I was intent on exhausting every possible avenue.

Weeks later, a wonderful lady named Rose at the Riverina Family History Group contacted me with good news. She had known the Harper and Wooding families, and was putting me in touch with Fred's niece Elvie and his nephew Allan because Fred and his siblings had passed away some years ago. Rose gave approximate dates. Not only that, but she also included information about the death and burial details of Hazel's baby brother, Edward, who had died while Hazel was in Parramatta Girls' Home. I was blown away because I hadn't asked for any of this, but it tied in with what I already had on file. To think that I had had so little information about my biological father, yet here I was, a couple of months after starting my search, and about to meet my cousins.

Rose thought it best that I contact Allan, whose mother was Fred's sister, because Elvie wasn't well at the time. My letter was dated 4 August 2002. In it I mentioned the circumstances of my birth, the search for my biological family, and my contact with Rose. I also wrote that Kevin and I would be visiting the Riverina soon, and asked if it would be possible to meet Allan.

The following week Kevin answered a call. He turned to me, with his hand over the receiver.

'It's your cousin, Allan.'

Nervously, I grabbed the phone and mumbled a few words before Allan responded and put me at ease. His voice was sensitive, and strong. We talked for some twenty minutes, the details of which I cannot recall now, except for him saying that he was looking forward to meeting us. I was on cloud nine, wildly excited by the prospect of meeting some of my biological father's family.

There were so many coincidences in my life—and so many Allans. My adoptive father, then Lorraine's eldest son, and now, cousin Allan, and Fred's younger brother had also been an Allan. I thought it weird that four should have the same name, and not be spelt in the usual way.

But then what about having a sister called Lorraine. That was even more strange. As was the nickname I chose for my adoptive father. As soon as *The Flintstones* came on TV in the early sixties, I began calling Allan 'Fred', and he called me 'Barney'. Even Flo used to laugh at us, when Allan and I tried to perfect our Fred and Barney voices.

More and more I began feeling like a detective, as well as a family historian although none of this would have been possible, of course, without Rose.

It had been September 1981 when I first met Hazel. Now, twenty-one years later, in September 2002, Kevin and I drove to the Riverina. It was bucketing down outside our camper trailer. We were staying in the caravan park for two nights but it was hard to relax. The same old insecurities began to surface. What if my new relatives didn't believe who I said I was and asked for proof? There was a blank space where Fred's name should have been on my birth certificate. Maybe it was irrational but I found this omission insulting. It was as if Fred didn't exist, as if Hazel didn't know who fathered her child, as if the child–me–didn't have any rights to know her father.

We phoned Allan and his wife Wendy soon after arriving.

'You must come and have lunch with us tomorrow,' said Wendy.

'What time?' I asked, accepting their invitation.

It was hard to sleep that night, and not because of the rain. I had intended to phone Rose after speaking with Allan and Wendy, but I was too excited to think straight.

The following morning we arranged to meet Rose at her place before heading off to Allan and Wendy's. This lady was so generous with both her time and information that we felt compelled to meet and thank her. Her warmth and hospitality was just exceptional.

By the time we arrived at my cousin's place and dashed down the concrete drive our shoes were saturated. We hastily removed them on the front verandah and rang the doorbell. It was almost midday. Allan was at work but would be home for lunch any minute, said Wendy, opening the door and inviting us in. I could see she was nervous but so were we. I am not sure who hugged who first, but it felt good, and we were soon at ease with each other. On the kitchen table were three black-and-white photographs. I hurried over and picked them up, knowing immediately who I was looking at.

'Is this...?'

'Yes,' said Wendy, 'that's Fred.'

I was so engrossed in Fred's picture that I hadn't noticed Allan coming in the door. He was only a few feet away when I looked up and saw him, grinning like a boy. He touched me gently on the shoulder, then bent down and kissed me on the cheek. I could see he was tall like Fred must have been. There were tears in Allan's eyes, and I was deeply touched by this lovely man and his wife accepting Kevin and me into their home as part of the family. I remember sitting around the table later, and being introduced to Elvie, Allan's eldest sister, and their Koori mate, John. I felt so at home, even before Elvie started talking about Fred.

He had fought in Papua New Guinea during the Second World War, on the Kokoda Track, she thought. In the late 1940s he had worked as a wharfie in Sydney and was still working there when he died. Elvie's face lit up, as she shared this memory of her uncle, my father.

'His shoes were so shiny you could almost see your face in them. And when he came to stay with us, which wasn't often, he used to clean my shoes, They were the shiniest at school.'

Looking at the full-length photo I could see what she meant. I liked what I saw of my father, of his family.

I was buoyant with joy. There was much to celebrate when we arrived home. Anyone who came to our house—and I invited lots of friends—had to reach around Fred and Hazel for the salt and pepper and the champagne glasses. Their photos were the centre of attention in their specially bought, double frame. I thought of Lorraine. If only she were here to see the similarity between her and Fred. But perhaps I was just imagining it because I wanted us to have the same father and be the twins that we joked we were.

I carted Fred's photo around for the next couple of months until I got used to the idea of him being a part of my life—but I still had to learn who he was, beyond his name and the fact that he was my father. Thanks to help from my cousin Allan I was able to access Fred's war service record, birth and marriage certificates. I sent copies of all to Allan. There was no mention of Kokoda, only Papua New Guinea. Some of the official Army handwriting was difficult to understand, complicated by military terminology. What did this abbreviation mean? And what about that one? One thing seemed clear though: Fred didn't appear to be a well man while in PNG, certainly not well enough to fight in a war.

To think my father had been in Papua New Guinea! The very idea gave me goose bumps. I had lived in Port Moresby when I was about the same age as Fred when he was there. Maybe I had walked in his footsteps. I'd visited the War Cemetery at Bomana, been to the foot of the Kokoda Track and spent a night in Rouna Falls, all three sites in close proximity to each other. Did Fred think of Hazel or me while he was up there? Did Hazel even tell him he had a daughter or two? She never said.

But the more I learnt about my father the more I wanted to learn. Surely there was someone who had worked with him on the wharves, or been with him in the 25th Battalion in 1943. I knew he'd been in either Milne Bay or Kokoda.

His death certificate led me to the site of his grave. It was in the Catholic section, where his mother was buried, at Botany Cemetery not far from La Perouse. As soon as we knew which cemetery, Kevin keyed the details in on the internet and hey presto, we had a map. Without this we would never have found him, because this cemetery is huge.

Unfortunately, Fred had died in 1970 at Fairfield Hospital, the same year I started nursing in Croydon. But I wasn't expecting him to be in an unmarked grave. I wept, and wondered if he died alone. I'd learned from his marriage certificate that his wife, Dorothy, who had been married twice before was much older than him and had died in 1956 of coronary disease. So Fred was a widower at thirty-eight years of age. But I still had no idea how Hazel knew he'd died. Had they kept in touch, like Jack and I had?

One of the first things Hazel told me when we met in 1981 was that Fred had died years back, but I had found it too hard to believe. Had she or anyone else in the family attended his funeral, I wanted to know. And I didn't understand why there wasn't a plaque at least, or some other acknowledgment of Fred's war service.

Now, in Botany Cemetery, I walked backwards and forwards, talking to him, this man who had given me life and whose bones lay buried in the soil right next to where I was standing. This was the closest I would ever get to my father. So much remained unsaid. I promised him I'd return with flowers.

My quest to learn all that I could about my father was compelling. Every avenue had to be explored. I wanted to know where had he lived. Maybe he'd had a neighbour who remembered him. I contacted the State Archives and checked out schools in the Riverina area. His name was on the records for 1926 at Mt Erin Catholic school in Wagga Wagga, but that was all.

My next task was to look for something in print about the waterfront. The first book I found—*Life on the Waterfront*—contained a photo of Jack, a good friend of Allan's. I was surprised but delighted to see his happy face smiling back at me. This Jack had also been a wharfie and had lived in the same block of flats in Redfern as my adoptive father. Tas Bull, the author, was formerly a seafarer, a wharfie, and a trade unionist of many years' standing, renowned in Australia and internationally. Not only did I appreciate his style of writing but he obviously cared deeply about human rights and social justice. I was so impressed by his autobiography I decided to write and thank him. Back to the electoral roll I went and there he was. In my letter I mentioned my search. I sent a scanned photo of Fred. Had Tas ever met him, I asked.

On 15 January 2003, I received a call from Tas. No, he couldn't recall meeting Fred, but there was to be a wharfies' reunion early in February. Tas would take Fred's photo along to see if anyone remembered working with him.

While waiting to hear from Tas I contacted the Army, the RSL, the War Memorial in Canberra, the Secretary of the 25th Battalion (that went to Kokoda), and later placed an advertisement in *Vetaffairs*, the Veteran Affairs newspaper, asking the same old question: did anyone know Fred Harper?

A few days after the reunion, Tas phoned me and apologised. None of the wharfies remembered Fred. So he would be sending Fred's photo back, with a copy of his Waterside Workers' Federation membership payments which included an Aboriginal Levy. This was a compulsory deduction for all workers, he said. It didn't have anything to do with my mother being Aboriginal. He didn't elaborate—and I didn't think to ask how the levy was spent and what group or organisation it went to. I was just grateful for any snippet of information about my father. I was hoping to meet with Tas to thank him personally, and to ask more about that levy, but in May 2003 he died suddenly and unexpectedly. So my question went unanswered.

Despite all my enquiries about Fred's war service, the only information that I could glean was that he had served in Milne Bay, suffered ill-health while in Papua New Guinea and probably shouldn't have been sent there. I learnt all this from an ex-digger who in September 2005, responded to my advertisement and generously offered to decipher Fred's war service record for me.

Your Dad wasn't a well man, and shouldn't have been sent to Papua New Guinea. He wasn't in Kokoda, but in Milne Bay, that's

> *where I was Love, but I didn't know your father personally. His battalion backed ours up—we couldn't have managed without them, the fighting was fierce. Do you mind if I keep the photo you sent me? We have become firm friends, your Dad and me.*

I am pleased to say that this old digger and I kept in touch.

In the weeks that followed my visit to Botany Cemetery, I cried buckets. It seemed strange to be grieving for someone I hadn't met, yet felt so attached to. Oh the lies, the lies. This was the man I'd been told was Afro-American. If Hazel hadn't told me that Fred was white I might never have learnt the truth. I really didn't care what nationality or race my father was, but the deception was very hard to forgive.

Parramatta Girls' Home

Blinded by the joy of feeling connected to my grandparents and Joe's open-armed welcome that made me feel I belonged, it took some years for me to see through the smoke screen of his supposed care and concern, and recognise my grandfather as a man of his times, in denial of how things really were. If Joe had only taken the time to use the same open-armed approach with Hazel as he had for me, her life might have turned out differently. In fact, this is what she alluded to when defending her unruly behaviour as a teenager, by saying that she only wanted to win her father's love and approval. It was generally agreed by family that Hazel was spoilt as a young child but this waned as other children arrived on the scene.

The difficulty I had with being the recipient of Joe's ongoing warmth was that I was receiving something that rightfully should have been given to my mother. For years I had been thinking about Parramatta Girls' Home and wondering how I could access that hellhole of a place to see it for myself, to gain an insight into what my mother had been through. But it wasn't until June 2003 that an opportunity presented itself.

I was watching television when Quentin Dempster's *Stateline* on the ABC (Australian Broadcasting Corporation, NSW) began. A program about Parramatta Girls' Home and its former inmates was on; this short documentary had been advertised for days beforehand. The camera panned back and forth, showing four Aboriginal women walking through the Home. I recognised two of them. The older lady, Aunty Marjorie Woodrow had been an inmate at the same time as Hazel. I learned later that Aunty Marjorie, Coral Pombo, plus a few others, had been instrumental in getting this program on air.

Aunty Marjorie and I had already met a couple of times through Link-Up. She thought she remembered my mother, but couldn't be sure.

'It was a long time ago, love,' she said.

I was so disappointed. I wanted someone to have been there, to have in some small way borne witness to my mother's pain.

Tearfully I watched these courageous women reliving their experiences. They too had been young girls, just like Hazel. So much brutality and rape lay behind those concrete walls. Out of sight, out of mind. It was worse than I had ever imagined. Their suffering was at the hands of sadists and a system that allowed terrible things to happen.

Not long after the program was screened an open day was

organised at Parramatta for all who had been inside, both black and white. Each woman was allowed to take one person with them. A Koori friend, Veronica, and I were doing it for our mothers who had both died. Kevin came with me.

Hazel had told me very little of what she had been through. Walking through this place, I now had some idea why. She had been shamed into silence, just like when she'd had me out of wedlock. It was common for girls not to tell anyone what they'd been through; even their families didn't know, some didn't want to know. I felt I was walking on eggshells, aware that I was moving over ground where many young girls and women had suffered and gone on suffering long afterwards. I already knew I'd come back. Once would never be enough. There were so many stories about girls being shoved into a dungeon area, bashed and raped. Was my mother one of them? And what was the operation she had undergone?

In December 2003, I was fortunate enough to be included in a four-day Aboriginal Women's Reunion for former inmates of the Parramatta Girls' Home. After the program had gone to air, Coral Pombo responded to an advertisement I had placed in the *Koori Mail* enquiring if anyone knew Hazel while she was in the home. Coral was too young to have known my mother, but she made contact and invited me to join her and the rest of the women, to do it for Hazel. It was a very generous offer, and I was delighted to accept.

During those four days we were tucked away in the bush at Picton in the Southern Highlands of NSW. One morning we travelled up to Sydney by bus to the Old Albion Street Children's Court in Surry Hills, where the welfare department used to take the girls to appear before the Magistrate for sentencing. Our second port of call was to Bidura in Glebe, now a Children's Court. Bidura replaced the Girls' Shelter in Avon Street, Glebe, which is mentioned in my mother's departmental file notes.

On our next trip we visited Parramatta and this time I was better prepared emotionally. Where was the dungeon I'd heard so much about? Was it the shower block or this poky dark place we were now standing in? Not only was I thinking about Hazel, but I was also remembering Flo's threats. If I didn't behave myself, this was where I might end up. It was a sobering thought.

Childless

Strangely for me, my search for my identity has been caught up with my feelings about motherhood. I cannot speak or write about one without mentioning or thinking of the other. They are so closely entwined at times it's embarrassing. It is as though I am always explaining myself. If it's not about identity, it's about having children.

Whenever I think about motherhood, I remember the conversation with Allan and Flo that night in March 1968 when the world as I knew it fell apart. Gone was my short-lived happiness with Jack—and with it any thoughts of marriage or motherhood. Many women of my generation seemed terrified of being left on the shelf. Some grabbed the first bloke that came along. We were expected to marry and to have a family by the time we were thirty. Those of us who didn't were treated as oddities. We still are in some quarters.

'How many children and grandchildren do you have?' people ask me.

'None,' I reply.

'Did you ever think of adopting?'

These questions used to puzzle me. Why would I adopt? I was able to have my own, I simply chose not to, though the choice was anything but simple.

I often wonder what Mrs Crane from Waverley Station would have made of my current situation, had she been alive today. Would she have reminded me of that eight-year-old who mothered anyone younger or smaller? Would she have understood my decision, or been aghast like Louie from Lifeline had in 1981 when he learnt that I was still alone and childless at thirty-eight?

So where did this decision not to have children stem from when I wanted nothing more than to be a mother? Can it be traced back as far as Crown Street Women's Hospital where my biological mother and I parted company? Or what about those first early weeks spent at Scarba Home?

During the search for my roots I had heard from a number of sources that Scarba was a terrible place for children to be. As I write that down now I pose the question I have asked myself many times over: is it possible, is it really possible for newborn babies to sense abandonment? Some research suggests that it is. A social worker once told me that abandonment at such a young age can be a loss some people never recover from.

From Scarba I was taken to live in Marrickville. My adoptive mother had always wanted a baby girl but cried when she got me home. I was that small she didn't know if she had a baby or a skinned rabbit, she told Allan.

I was eight months old when I was handed over each working day to Allan's older sister, Winnie, so Flo could go back to work at the woollen mills. I say 'handed over' because years later Winnie made it clear she didn't like me. I wasn't a blood relative, and when it came to my dirty nappies well, as far as she was concerned, you could smell them and me a mile off.

This childcare arrangement continued until I was two years old, old enough for kindergarten, as it was called then. Allan told me there were days when Flo forgot to pick me up. He blamed it on the lure of the American servicemen who were in town a lot during those days in 1945, and Flo was an attractive woman. Other members of the family were dragged in to take responsibility for me and I think I sensed as a toddler that I was a problem to the adults around me. Perhaps this was why Allan decided to move his family to Walgett, to get Flo away from all the temptations of city life.

My imaginary friends drove my mother mad. She had work to do, she'd get nothing done at this rate, she said. There was no-one to play with. I was a curious child and I wanted a brother or sister more than anything. Allan and I became the best of friends—I followed him everywhere. But despite loving him, I never lost that deep hunger I had for a mother's love. I would often tell Flo that I loved her, but though she smiled, she was quick to push me away.

'Don't be silly,' she would say.

Once I'd moved to Sydney, on those occasions when I was out with my cousin, I would wish that someone kind would come along and take me home with them. I wasn't interested in boys or teenage parties. I had only just turned eleven and didn't know how to behave. I was sending out mixed signals, crying out for love, and pulling back as soon as anyone showed interest. Men were only after one thing, I decided, especially men like creepy Uncle Ernie. How did my aunt put up with him, I ask myself now.

'That's why you grew up so quick, and feel older. You had to mother yourself,' said Louie, at one of our counselling sessions.

Even Allan told people that I brought myself up. It made me cringe, because he seemed proud of me doing what he and Flo should have done.

By the time I was a teenager, Flo and I were getting along much better. Maybe because I wasn't at home as much. Sometimes, before I had turned eighteen, Flo, Allan and I would have a drink together at the Robin Hood Hotel. I enjoyed Flo's company better than Allan's then, because she was fun to be with. I didn't like being seen with both at once. I was trying to break free, and also fantasising about what it would be like to be a mother myself. I'd noticed the way my best friend's brother, Jimmy, looked at me, but if I'd mentioned this to Flo, she would have said that I had tickets on myself. Other people didn't say this though, they seemed to like me. It was as if I were unworthy of my mother's love, but it didn't stop me loving her, or being grateful that she adopted me. Who knows where I would have ended up if she hadn't. In my early adult years I blamed myself. I must have expected too much from my mother, I decided. Maybe there were many adoptees who experienced this feeling of not being worthy of a mother's love.

When I found my family at the age of thirty-eight, the connecting process had taken a bigger toll than I imagined. Somewhere along the line what had once been a strong sense of abandonment, and a desire to be a mother, became a firm decision not to have children, not to take that risk. Some people from such a background may wish to have a child so that they can restore the balance, give to that child what they'd never had themselves. In my case, my empathy was also with the unborn child, but in a different way. I didn't—or couldn't—trust that I wouldn't continue a cycle of abuse and neglect. I was also anxious that my child might be taken away from me just as I had been taken from my mother.

I can look back now and see that though I wasn't fully conscious of my actions that New Year's Eve in 1969, when I finally broke off with Jack, it was as though I put my foot on some unseen umbilical cord. At the time my reasoning was simple: if I couldn't have Jack's child, then I didn't want anyone else's.

I wasn't to know these feelings would change when I met Kevin in 1982. When I didn't conceive within a certain time, we had tests done. Kevin said the results didn't bother him either way, but he was more disappointed for me, than himself. For years

I regretted and struggled against that earlier decision but I never did trust anyone enough to lift my foot from that stranglehold on motherhood. Some part of me, wiser than my conscious mind, made the decision then, and this I believe, prevented me having a complete breakdown as a young woman.

And then in August 1991, Lorraine died and I knew I needed to write.

Lorraine

The writing down of the story of my life has been an important part of my healing process. It was 1991, and I was forty-eight, when my feelings began pouring onto the page, in poetry form. I didn't think of it as anything more than a conversation between my sister and me, an attempt to understand why she died when she did. Surely she wasn't supposed to die at forty-seven. All those plans we'd made. We were going to have fun, do sisterly things together. I was going to talk to her again about giving up smoking. She laughed when I'd tried the first time.

'Yeah, I know I should, but I'll probably be reaching for that one last smoke before they close the lid of the coffin.'

During the service at her funeral I was sure I saw Lorraine's hand coming out of that box. It was as if she were having the last laugh and trying to get me to laugh with her. After hearing that I was adopted and how alike Lorraine and I were, the minister kept asking me to give the eulogy. I would have liked nothing more but I was concerned about Jenny, our younger sister. She and Lorraine weren't on speaking terms when Lorraine died. And I didn't want to make Jenny feel worse than she probably did, because it was she who had grown up with Lorraine, not me. I was a Johnny-come-lately.

Lorraine had said that we were going to grow old together to make up for all the time we had missed during those early years. She was a breastfeeding mum at sixteen, and again at nineteen, and had had a miscarriage at twenty-three.

'It was a girl,' she said. 'I always wanted a girl, but I'm more than happy with my two boys. The only thing I regret was getting married at sixteen. I missed out on all the fun that teenagers are supposed to have.'

Had we met twenty years earlier, and had Aunty Pat spoken up I might have been a young mum like Lorraine. We had been talking about dressmaking one day. Aunty Pat made bridal gowns for a place in the city that specialised in weddings. I told her I used to make my own clothes as well, when I worked at Winn's Department Store in Blacktown.

'Did you really? That's where I used to buy my material before they closed down. Now that you mention it, I remember being served by a young girl and thinking to myself how she looked like Hazel and Lorraine. That was probably you, love.'

'Yeah, Aunty, it probably was. If only you had said something, eh.'

However, it was no longer 1961, but thirty years later, and I was struggling to cope with losing my sister. I thought her dying when she did was a cop-out. She had this special recipe for mushroom soup and was going to cook it for me. We also had tickets to see the Buddy Holly musical at Her Majesty's Theatre. We were going to bop along together, like teenagers and reclaim that part of our life.

A week after Lorraine died, I told Kevin that I didn't know how I'd manage without her. It was sometime before he replied.

'You know, you're very lucky.'

Lucky? How could losing Lorraine be lucky? What did he know? He hadn't lost any of his sisters, and he had six of them, as well as an older brother.

'What do you mean I'm lucky?'

'Some people go through their whole lifetime and never experience what you and Lorraine shared in the last six months that you had together.'

The evening that Lorraine fell ill, and just a few hours before she lapsed into unconsciousness, I had a strong feeling to talk to her. I wanted to tell her how much I loved her and how proud of her I was for achieving all that she had on her own. But I stopped myself from phoning her, as I had on many previous occasions.

Years before, Lorraine had warned me about getting too close and smothering her. I didn't think I was going overboard, but she thought I was and she stopped talking to me. She didn't say anything at the time, just stopped phoning and was abrupt whenever I phoned her. So I gave up, and I stopped calling her.

It was four years later when I finally decided to break the silence and a letter from Lorraine arrived in response to a birthday card I'd sent. I was happier than I'd been in years. Not only had she responded but she had included her work contact details, and the time she went to lunch. Surely this meant that all was forgiven. Not that there anything to forgive.

It was a few days before I made contact, I didn't want to stuff up again by appearing too eager. When I drove into her workplace, Lorraine was waiting at the front entrance wearing a big smile.

'It's good to see you again', she said, as I opened the car door.

'And you.'

'Come inside, I'll introduce you to my boss, he's lovely and even younger than my Allan. I'm learning to use a computer. Imagine that! I've never worked in an office before. I nearly died when they told me what I'd be doing.'

A lot was fitted into that lunchbreak, a lot of talking, catching up and being dragged around the office to meet this one and that one. It was so wonderful to be on good terms again, though I was a bit miffed when Lorraine remarked in front of her boss how grey I was compared to the last time she'd seen me four years ago. I noticed that she had a lot more wrinkles, but kept it to myself until we were alone.

'Yeah, I know, that's the smoking. It ages your skin.'

'Next time we have lunch, Lorraine, we'll talk about you giving it up,' I told her.

'Yeah. But you already know what I've told you about my last smoke.'

Here we were, bouncing off each other, like old times. Both of us looking forward to meeting again. And that's how it was for the next five months, until Lorraine lapsed into unconsciousness, and died.

It was some time before Kevin's words sank in. Lucky? I was sitting on the floor, laughing, crying, nodding and shaking my head as I sorted through bags of wool and half-finished hand-knitted jumpers, that had once belonged to Lorraine. We'd both knitted a lot over the years and considered ourselves pretty good at it.

Not long before Lorraine passed away she was told she was going to be a grandmother. This was the opportunity she'd been waiting for. She'd always wanted to learn how to knit ducks into baby jumpers and cardigans. Would I come with her, she asked. I was already enrolled in another course, learning how to knit lace, so I didn't have time. She promised to teach me once she knew what was what. And I would do the same and show her. After the first class she phoned me. Her duck looked nothing like a duck.

'More like a triangle,' she said, giggling into the phone.

'It couldn't be that bad. You're such a good knitter.'

'You should see it,' she said, starting both of us off again.

At 9pm the following night, Thursday, Jimmy, my brother-in-law went to bed. He had to be up early the next morning for work. Lorraine had to be up early as well but like me she was a night owl and stayed up till all hours.

Jimmy dozed on and off, looking at the clock every so often. When the light was still on in the lounge room and Lorraine hadn't come to bed by 1am, Jimmy thought he'd better investigate. And just as well he did, because there was Lorraine, unconscious on the lounge, with the television set still on.

At eight-thirty that morning, I had just arrived home, showered and was about to have breakfast after working night duty, when Jimmy phoned to tell me Lorraine had had a cerebral haemorrhage.

'Tell me it isn't true, Jimmy? She'll be all right, won't she?'

'Yes, love, it is true. She's in Intensive Care at Royal North Shore Hospital and will be operated on soon.'

The following day was Saturday, the day Lorraine and I were meant to be going to see the Buddy Holly show at Her Majesty's. She'd asked me to book and pay for the tickets. She was going to fix me up when we got there. I was trying to convince myself that she'd be all right. Some people were after a cerebral haemorrhage, weren't they? I hadn't nursed any, but one of my sister-in-laws said that she knew someone who hadn't suffered any ill effects from having hers, so maybe Lorraine would be one of the lucky ones. I was still banking on her coming with me that Saturday afternoon because Kevin wasn't a Buddy Holly fan. It was him who'd suggested I ask Lorraine in the first place.

I phoned Kevin after hearing Jimmy's bad news.

'Now you'll have to come with me,' I said.

I then contacted Jenny in Brisbane to let her know about Lorraine and told her that Kevin and I would pick her up from Mascot airport on Monday morning.

Kevin and I did go to see Buddy Holly. But despite moving in time to the music and singing along my heart wasn't in it, not with my precious sister on life support. Despite knowing how ill Lorraine was, part of me didn't want to believe it. She'd be okay, I kept telling myself. I hung onto these thoughts until I couldn't hang onto them any longer. My sister was going to die.

The next five days were fraught with emotion. Disbelief, shock, anger, regret, grief, laughter, tears and more tears, and finally acceptance. Lorraine had had a cerebral haemorrhage, due to a cerebral aneurysm. She was on life support. Her condition was deteriorating, and we were just waiting for Tommy to arrive from Queensland. Then it was time to say goodbye and for the respirator to be switched off. This was the first time I'd ever been with my mother and five siblings all at once. It should have been a happy occasion, this gathering of family, but the only time it was, was when Jenny suggested I have a cappuccino with Tommy on my own, because he and I had only met once before, and that was in February 1982, nine and a half years earlier. It was a lovely gesture of Jenny's, especially at a time like that.

Lorraine's funeral was the biggest I'd ever been to. I sat in the front pew with Tommy holding one hand and Wayne the other. Jeff and Jenny sat on the left of Tommy, and they too held hands throughout the service. I felt very sad for Hazel, and for my sisters, because they hadn't spoken to each other for most of their grown-up lives. Hazel was the only one in the family who didn't seem to have any time or love for her daughters, or her grand-daughters. The damage caused by harsh words and rejection had taken its toll. It was irreparable and I found it heartbreaking to witness.

When my sisters were teenagers and needed their mother the most, Hazel was nowhere to be found. Maybe she needed some mothering of her own. No wonder my sisters married so young. I probably would have too given the same set of circumstances. Both Lorraine and Jenny refused to bad-mouth our mother; they had wanted me to have the chance to get to know Hazel before they said anything about her to me. I thought it was very considerate on their part, but Hazel wasn't so generous in return. However, despite the rift between her and Jenny, at least Hazel came to the hospital to say goodbye to Lorraine. It must have taken a lot of courage for her to do that—and to come to Lorraine's funeral.

Lorraine told me there was no way she could have maintained an ongoing relationship with our family, not with Hazel playing wedge politics. Consequently, in one of our heart-to-hearts she expressed her sense of abandonment. Yes, there were those like her stepmother and Aunty Pat who taught her how to knit and care for her newborn baby, but they weren't around for very long.

'What I needed was a mother, one I could call my own,' she said.

Lorraine had confided in me that she had a similar experience to mine as a young girl in regards to a male relative, and that Hazel hadn't believed her, just as Flo had been dismissive of me. It's strange when I think about it now because Hazel told me about this on the very first day we met. I was too shocked to reply.

Two months after Lorraine died, my brother Tommy invited me to attend his daughter Jodie's wedding outside Toowoomba in Queensland. I hadn't seen my niece since she was twelve years old. She was now twenty and the spitting image of Lorraine at the same age, like two peas in a pod, her beauty and spontaneity a joy to behold. I would have felt privileged to call Jodie my daughter and her brother Paul my son. Lorraine lives on through our niece, and being at her wedding helped soften the blow of losing my beloved sister.

Kevin was right. I was lucky. I am lucky. Lucky to have found my family, and lucky to have discovered my Aboriginality. Lucky to have had Lorraine, and lucky to have Kevin in my life. Lucky and grateful.

As I worked my way through Lorraine's knitting bag, a few weeks after she had died, I laughed to myself. This was another thing we had in common. Neither of us could see the need to finish one jumper before starting another. Not if we saw other wool that we liked better. We could have a few things on the go at the same time. That way we didn't get bored.

I was sitting on the carpet in the bedroom, laughing, crying and talking to my sister. 'Who was this beautiful sky-blue jumper for?' I asked. Anyone could have worn it. There was nothing to say it was for a man or a woman. There was another jumper and an apple-green cardigan in Bluebell crepe, with a lacy pattern, the one she'd been telling me about. It was for herself and almost finished except for a sleeve. There was an assortment of odd booties in varying shades of pink, and a bonnet. If only she could have lived to see her first grandchild, a boy, born seven months after she had died. Lorraine's boys were her life, as were their wives. Had she been alive today, Lorraine would have been a proud grandmother of two boys and two girls.

I continued to rummage and pulled out a small knitted square. What was this weird-looking triangle thing in the middle? I started to giggle. Could this possibly be the duck?

Writing

It was the early nineties when I first came across the *Koori Mail.* Towards the back was an advertisement asking Aboriginal or Torres Strait Islander people who were interested in doing a two-year Associate Diploma Course in Adult Education (Koori Ed) to fill in the application form and send it off to the University of Technology, in Sydney. The course not only appealed to me, but it seemed the only way of me getting into university with the minimal education that I had from school.

After fifteen years of nursing, I'd had enough. It was time for a career change. My aim was to learn as much as I could about Aboriginal History, get a tertiary degree and maybe teach in the field. The good thing about this course was that it was in block release mode.

The students, mostly mature-age from country, city and interstate, came together every six weeks or so for a week or two before going back to their communities. Lectures, field trips and assignments were spread over those two years. The time went quickly and I graduated with the rest of our group at the end of 1993. Encouraged by this, and by comments from some of the lecturers, I applied for and was accepted to do a BA in Communications, majoring in Aboriginal Studies and Writing, full-time.

It was full on from that very first day. It was a struggle just to keep up, but it was exciting, challenging and stimulating. I was fifty-one years of age, and surrounded by bright, intelligent people. Many had just finished their HSC. Some would ask what I was doing after class, and if I'd like to have coffee with them. They thought I'd done so much with my life compared to theirs.

There were lots of mature-age students as well, including a number of Kooris; we were mutually supportive and enjoyed each other's company. We would congregate before class at Zac's Coffee Shop in Harris Street, to compare assignments and stew over presentations, a task I was terrified of and never did master. But I wasn't going to let that stop me from getting through first year.

In early 1995 I had just enrolled for second year when something inside me said, 'I can't—and don't want to—write about anyone or anything but me. And I need to do it now.'

'Defer for twelve months,' said a couple of my lecturers. 'Don't leave, Lorraine, you might regret it.'

So, defer, I did.

They say everyone has a book in them. Up until dropping out of uni and beginning to seriously write I hadn't really thought of my life as a narrative. But working my way through this manuscript as I did on and off for twelve or more years, forced me to take a closer look and ask myself exactly why had I said this or done that. Because of such scrutiny I have become aware of—and been struck by—the amount of running, emotionally and physically, I have done from my earliest days. Not just on the track, but other kinds too—running from relationships, running from life, running from my life. This has cost me dearly over the years.

Sharing life stories—either orally or in written form—helps to dispel fear and enlighten people, or at least that is what is intended and hoped. Yet there are those who no matter how many times they hear stories about identity and what it means to be Indigenous in contemporary Australia seem unable or unwilling to rid themselves of the stereotypical views of Aboriginal people that many have been carrying around in their heads for decades.

'You don't look Aboriginal,' people keep saying to me. 'You must take after the white side of your family.'

My identity is not so difficult a concept to grasp. It's not as if I'm trying to claim something that isn't rightfully mine. When someone says they are Australian, Italian, Korean or whatever this isn't disputed. They know who they are, the same as I know who I am. There isn't just one look that defines a race of people, and that goes for Indigenous people of Australia as well. My descendants are English, Irish and Aboriginal, but it is the Aboriginal roots that were denied me, and for which I have been discriminated against. Perhaps this is why they mean the most to me.

~

In the mid-1990s, following publication of some of my poetry, I was asked to speak to various reconciliation groups, and invited to read my work at a number of public events. I carried photos with me to these sessions, selected images of myself as a child and young adult, showing how I looked more stereotypically Aboriginal when I was younger. I saw these pictures as proof of my identity, my Aboriginality.

'See,' I would exclaim, hating myself more each time for resorting to this defensive kind of statement.

There were times though when even these images failed to convince some individuals. Crestfallen, I'd persist in justifying and explaining myself. There have been occasions too, when I have had to justify myself to some Kooris, because they think I'm not dark enough, or don't fit a particular mould. Usually though, once I explain that I was taken from my mother, there is understanding. My individual story fits against the backdrop of a much larger picture.

Now, in my later years, it seems that I look like anyone else in this multicultural country. I certainly don't stand out anymore,

I have blended in. A good thing too, you might say, but can you grasp how much harder that has made it to reconnect with my roots? Can you imagine how complex it can be trying to prove aspects of identity to people who persist in misunderstanding—or resisting—what I am talking about?

When I have been asked to share my story with some group or other, I have discussed the issue of identity and talked about the government's definition of an Aboriginal or Torres Strait Islander person. But there has always been someone who, despite having everything explained, will sidle up to me afterwards and say, 'Yes but, you don't look Aboriginal.'

It seems ironic that in my childhood when I was black, I wanted to be white like everyone else. And now, when I want to acknowledge my Aboriginality, I'm taken for a Caucasian. I once heard an academic express the view that this inability or resistance by non-Indigenous people to understand the concept of Indigenous identity has to do with resentment of the perceived special treatment and benefits that Indigenous people receive from the government.

In some people's eyes, the darker an Aboriginal or Torres Strait Islander person is, the more Indigenous they are. Hence, they are more entitled to benefits, and more entitled to claim their identity.

I often hear these views expressed in the media and in the community. I would like to have worked out ways to respond to questions about my Aboriginality by now, but the truth is that they still take me by surprise. I just don't get it.

During a camping holiday around Australia some years ago, I met two Elders who came from Oombulgurri Mission, which was previously known as Forrest River Mission. Oombulgurri is north-west of and just across the Cambridge Gulf from Wyndham, in Western Australia. One man said that he'd been taken away, while the other remarked that his wife was a half-caste like me. Being called a half-caste in this context didn't bother me, because this is how light-skinned Aboriginals are spoken about in this part of the country, where black skin dominates. And this man wasn't some ten-year-old kid in the 1950s from Isis River, speaking out of ignorance and bigotry. I didn't have to explain myself to him because he understood.

Had Lorraine been alive today, what advice might she have given me?

'If anyone asks who you are, say you're Aboriginal. I do,' she said, soon after we met in 1982.

'It doesn't matter what other people think, you don't have to explain yourself to them. You know who you are, and why you did what you did. And that's your business, not theirs.'

Epilogue

It wasn't until Prime Minister Kevin Rudd announced the date of the Apology to members of the Stolen Generations on behalf of the Australian government—Wednesday, 13 February 2008—that I began to sit up and take notice. Up till this point I'd ruled out the possibility of saying 'sorry' ever happening. I knew full well that an apology would never happen under the previous Howard government. Besides, they didn't need to say sorry to me. It was my grandfather who was responsible for my removal, not any racist government policy. For the past eleven years this had been my mantra, but suddenly things were different. A change was in the air.

Kevin and I were in Port Stephens when we heard the news. I'd been so consumed with my own grief and loss that I'd forgotten my mother's, my grandmother's, my brothers', sisters' and extended family members', and that of all the other mothers, fathers and families who had suffered—and continue to suffer—because of past policies of removal of Indigenous children.

This apology wasn't just about me–or whether I was or wasn't a Stolen Generations member. It was much more than that. It was about acknowledging past wrongs that had been done in this country, including the telling of gross lies when it came to the adoption of Aboriginal babies. And as far as I was concerned, saying sorry was the right and proper thing to do if healing and reconciliation were to take place.

~

In the years between 1997 and 2002 many things, including the writing of this book, took a back seat in my life. Largely this was because of what was happening 'out there' in this country, both socially and politically. It drove me to seek out like-minded people who were interested in addressing social justice and human rights issues, especially for Indigenous peoples. What had triggered this off for me in April 1997 was Sir Ronald Wilson handing down to Federal Parliament the *Bringing Them Home* report of the National Inquiry into the Separation of Aboriginal and Torres Strait Islander Children from their Families.

I was one of the people who the previous year had been asked to put a submission in. So I was very interested in knowing the outcome and how it would be received by the conservative Howard government. 'Dismissive' is the word that springs to mind. I was initially gutted by the government's response. Then I was outraged that these glaring issues of Indigenous disadvantage and government neglect could be denied. Fortunately, others in the community were expressing their outrage as well. And soon, Kevin and I were meeting lots of gutsy, articulate and good people, the kind I'd been searching for all my life. They weren't relaxed and comfortable with what was happening either. We had to do something about it, we agreed, and started spreading the word.

The Lane Cove Residents for Reconciliation was born on 14 February 1998 and it wasn't long before there were many other reconciliation groups across Australia, all with similar ideals. I am very happy to call myself a co-founder of this group, along with Kerrie McKenzie and all of our hard-working executive committee. We have had support from our local council and over the years have received awards for our reconciliation work in the community and with schools.

Late in January 2008, not long before Kevin Rudd's Apology, I was told that I had won the Inaugural Yabun Elder of the Year Award. It was one of five awards presented to Indigenous people in recognition of their contributions over the past twelve months within the Koori Radio 93.7FM footprint of the Sydney, Central Coast, Blue Mountains and Wollongong regions. My award was for my commitment to reconciliation and the involvement I'd had over the years with Lane Cove Council and in the community. I was stunned when I received the call.

'But no-one knows who I am,' I muttered.

'They will now,' was the reply.

The ceremony at the Australia Council for the Arts in Surry Hills on 22 January 2008 was the most touching I had ever been to. It was a such special day.

~

Three and a bit weeks later there was no way Kevin and I could not go to Canberra. Nothing was going to stop us, or so we thought until we were just outside Goulburn the evening before. We heard a sudden whoosh. It was a tyre blow-out. It had been ten years since we'd had a flat, let alone a blow-out, and consequently the nuts on the spare tyre wouldn't budge. Not only that, our jack wouldn't work properly. There'd been rain showers on the way down and now it was cloudy and the light was fading, It was nail-biting time. Would we make it to Canberra?

'Yes, of course we will.'

Just then a young man pulled up behind us. He was used to changing tyres, he said. He didn't muck around, the wheel was off and on in no time. We thanked him, and promised ourselves that when we got back home we'd make sure to fix these things up so that they worked when we needed them.

After spending the night in Goulburn, we were up bright and early and soon on our way. It was just a hundred kilometres to Canberra. Kevin decided to drop me as close to Parliament House as he could manage and then go off in search of tyres. By now it was 7.30am, less than two hours to go before the Prime Minister's address to the nation. Kevin was sure he'd be back in time. He wanted to share this momentous occasion with me. In the meantime, we would keep in touch by mobile phone. He kissed me and off he went. I asked someone the way to Parliament House.

'Just follow that path,' the woman said.

I looked up towards the big white building on the hill, where the bigwigs and invited guests would be. I pulled my lightweight jacket closer and zipped it up. I couldn't stop shivering. If only my mother, brothers, sisters and other family could be here. If only Kevin were here. I felt very alone and empty-headed, as if none of it was real. But I just followed groups of people carrying blankets, baskets, babies, banners and flags—the Aboriginal flag, the Torres Strait Islander flag and the one with the Union Jack on it.

I found a large grassy area and grabbed two white plastic chairs. I carried them two rows from the front, wiping the moisture off before sitting down. There were two big screens facing me. The place was filling up. I hoped I would meet someone I knew, I needed to talk. I knew that Kerrie McKenzie was somewhere in Canberra, maybe already here in the crowd, and there'd be people from other reconciliation groups here too. It wasn't as if I wouldn't know anyone. But I was getting anxious, it was 8.30am. Where was Kevin?

~

I look around to see if I can spot anyone I know. There's what's-her-name from that reunion for former inmates at Parramatta Girls' Home. In my haste to catch her before she moves on I knock my chair over. I remember her name just in time. Rachael Walker. There's a fella with her.

Suddenly Rachael remembers that she isn't alone and introduces me to her friend. Jack is from Cape York. And soon she's sitting on Kevin's chair next to me. I still haven't heard from Kevin. It's now after nine.

'When your hubby comes, I'll give the chair back,' Rachael promises.

The tension is building. The screens ahead are lighting up. Rachael hands me a beautiful red rose.

'One for your mother and one for mine. I'm so pleased you called out to me, Lorraine. Not everyone does.'

I reach for her hand. Rachael is a great poet and artist, at least that's what I think. I'd seen some of her work at the reunion when we were staying in the Southern Highlands for a few days. I couldn't understand why anyone would want to ignore Rachael.

I look up at the big screen in front of the crowd. The Speaker in the House is introducing the Prime Minister. Rachael squeezes my hand; this is what we've all been waiting for. A loud cheer goes up. At some stage we're on our feet along with everyone else, clapping, cheering, crying, clapping, laughing, thanking our Prime Minister. Hugging and kissing each other.

Then my mobile rings. It's Kevin, still at the garage, ten kilometres away. He's tried to contact me several times but keeps getting a recorded message. He'll see me soon.

It's 10.30am by now. I don't know who spots who first, but it's my two cousins, Ian and Harold, brothers. Harold had dark hair when I'd met him at Wallaga Lake for the first time fourteen years ago. I haven't seen him since, and now he's greyer than me, with a grey goatee beard. I don't recognise him at first.

'Who's this fella?' I keep asking Ian.

'My brother, Harold. You know Harold?'

We can't stop talking, laughing and hugging each other.

'This is my family,' I tell anyone who'll listen. 'My family.'

Some give me doubtful looks, but what does it matter if my skin is light and my cousins are dark. They know who I am and where I fit in, and I know who they belong to and how we are related. And that's all that counts.

'Lorraine darling, would you like your photo taken with your family?' asks Lizzie Landers, one of my reconciliation friends and a member of the Manly Warringah Pittwater Aboriginal Support Group that dates back to the late 1970s.

'Yes please.'

My mobile rings again.

'Where are you?'

And a moment later Kevin's beside me.

'Sorry,' he gasps.

Now it's our turn for a hug. Soon we'll go and get something to eat and drink.

Postscript

Shortly after receiving an advance copy of *Hey Mum, What's a Half-Caste?* a long held family secret came to light. The truth is my maternal grandfather was Aboriginal, the same as my much-loved grandmother who took this secret to her grave. Perhaps she was in fear of being judged. This revelation provided answers to the many issues that arose whilst researching my book.

Lorraine McGee-Sippel

Bibliography

Bringing them Home: Report of the National Inquiry into the Separation of Aboriginal and Torres Strait Islander Children from their Families, Human Rights and Equal Opportunity Commission, Sydney, 1997

Bull, Tas, *Life on the Waterfront: an autobiography*, Harper Collins, NSW, 1998

Edwards, Coral and Read, Peter (eds), *The Lost Children*, Doubleday, Sydney, 1989

Kendall, Carol, *Link-Up Booklet*, Link-up New South Wales Aboriginal Corporation, NSW

Tucker, Margaret, *If Everyone Cared: autobiography of Margaret Tucker*, Ure Smith, Sydney, 1977

Valentine, Carolyn and Slaytor, Petrina, *Down the Track – Outcomes of Adoptions Reunions*, NSW Committee on Adoption, Sydney, 1990